WITHDRAWN

Mary Elizabeth Haldane

WITHDRAWN

MY MOTHER IN HER NINETIETH YEAR.
From a Sketch by James Paterson, R.S.A., P.R.S.W.

Mary Elizabeth Haldane

A RECORD OF A HUNDRED YEARS

(1825-1925)

EDITED BY HER DAUGHTER
[ELIZABETH SANDERSON HALDANE]
WITH NOTES BY HER ELDEST SON
[RICHARD BURDON SANDERSON,
VISCOUNT HALDANE],
ADDITIONAL CONTRIBUTIONS,
AND LINES WRITTEN BY A GRAND-DAUGHTER
[NAOMI MITCHISON]
WITH AN INTRODUCTION
BY THE ARCHBISHOP OF YORK

Kennedy & Boyd
an imprint of
Zeticula
57 St Vincent Crescent
Glasgow
G3 8NQ
Scotland.

http://www.kennedyandboyd.co.uk
admin@kennedyandboyd.co.uk

First published in 1926
This Edition Copyright ©
Estate of Naomi Mitchison 2009.

ISBN-13 978-1-84921-030-0 Paperback
ISBN-10   1-84921-030-6 Paperback

INTRODUCTION
by the
ARCHBISHOP OF YORK

When great personalities pass from our sight, it seems almost a duty to preserve some record of the place they filled and the influence they had in their own day and generation. It is, I imagine, because I pressed this duty upon Miss Haldane that the honour has been given to me of writing some words of introduction to this little book. It seemed to me only right that some account should be given of one whom I, in common with all who knew her, will ever regard as one of the most remarkable women of her time, and of the impression she made on those whom her life touched during its century of years.

The opening chapter gives a picture, all the more vivid because drawn with Mrs. Haldane's characteristic simplicity and directness, of the influences of her childhood. In the other chapters her daughter and her eldest son—with a self-restraint which their mother would have valued —have described her later life, and the influence which she had in her own home and among her many friends. It is always difficult to give a picture of any rich and strong personality, and the difficulty is especially great in the case of Mrs. Haldane. For her life, though full, was very quiet. Her powers were not shown in the activities of public life. She was so utterly free from any kind of self-consciousness that what she spoke or wrote was always entirely simple and unstudied. Thus neither the events of her life, nor her letters—written in her strong, clear handwriting, and expressed in language of severe simplicity yet of a certain old-world dignity—can really explain the influence she wielded or the impression she made. These were the result simply of personal contact with her own personality.

In these words of introduction I may be permitted to represent those who outside her own family circle had the privilege of knowing her or even of seeing her if only for a few moments. When we were admitted to her chamber of peace, and sat beside her, and heard her deep, musical voice, and watched the play of expression in her clear, calm eyes, we knew that we were in the presence of a spirit singularly noble, pure, and strong. We felt that she was living in the sphere of the eternal, in a region where the ultimate values of human life were consciously and constantly realized, in abiding and tranquil communion with God. She seemed to us instinctively to view men and events sub specie æternitatis, *from the point of view of the eternal.*

This outlook became ever more sure and steadfast as the years of her long life drew to a close. Old age was to her a period not of increasing weakness, but rather of ever-growing spiritual power. " As age advances," she wrote to me in her ninety-ninth year, " the certainty of God's presence and willingness to commune with us grows stronger and somehow ever more real as if there were but a step between

*time and eternity. I cannot altogether account
for it, but it grows stronger and stronger as age
advances." " Strange, is it not," she said to
me once, " that it has come to me after ninety-five
years of life to begin to realize the full meaning
of the words ' the gift of the Spirit is joy' ? "
And I have a very vivid recollection of her a few
years earlier, before she was finally confined to
her own room, standing candle in hand with the
light falling on her beautiful face, saying : " Some
bodily powers, I suppose, are going, but I begin
to feel moving within me in a way which I sometimes cannot understand ' the powers of the
world to come.' " I remembered then some
words whose source I have never been able to
trace—they are singularly applicable to Mrs.
Haldane—" She knew that she was growing old
not so much by the increasing weakness of the
body as by the increasing vitality of the soul."*

*It was this vivid and constant sense of the
eternal that gave her a large-hearted tolerance
of ways of thought and life very different from
her own. To the end she kept without doubt or*

question the strong simplicity of her own Christian faith. But in her nearness to the world of eternal values she realized that there are many ways of approach to that world—many symbols in which its ultimate truths can be expressed. With every mind which was sincere, every spirit which was in aim high and pure, she felt herself and the faith which she held to be akin.

Yet although living more and more in this sphere of the eternal, she kept to the last the most keen and vivid interest in the public affairs of her time as well as in the personal lives of her children, and grandchildren, and great-grand-children, and friends. This interest found, indeed, its highest and fullest expression in her prayers. Thus in the midst of the Great War she wrote : " In my quiet resting-place I can in my feebleness take hold of the Almighty power of our Father in Heaven to strengthen the arms, and I may add [a characteristic touch] the brains of those who are bearing in one way or another the strain and weight of the awful struggle in which we are engaged. These are ever present with me, and

b

*night and day it seems as if we never could fix
our thoughts on anything else in the world.
But yet I feel unshaken in my confidence that the
Lord Himself will be exalted and destroy the
power of wickedness on the earth." So, again,
with a quaint use of Old Testament imagery
with which she was so familiar, she was wont
to compare the Archbishops, whom she honoured
with her friendship, to the two golden candlesticks
of the tabernacle, and herself to one of the pipes
through which the oil was supplied for their light
in answer to constant prayer. This thought was
in her mind when she wrote to me the letter which
was the last she ever wrote with her own hand,
and which for this reason is printed at the end
of this book.*

*But let it not for a moment be supposed that
this steadfast ministry of prayer was her only
way of showing her constant interest in the things
of the world. She followed the course of events
and the careers of public men with the activity
of a strong and cultivated intellect. Thus I
remember finding her in her ninety-seventh year*

reading a bulky history of modern Europe because, as she said, the changes wrought by the Peace of Versailles and the account of foreign affairs in the newspapers were so complicated that she was compelled to go back to the history which lay behind them. And her judgments of men and policies and books were always well informed and often shrewd.

Moreover, her habitual elevation of mind and outlook was relieved from any austerity not only by her keen human interests, but also by a rich and quiet humour. It often came, like all true humour, unexpectedly. It was almost always kindly, but when directed towards any sort of boastfulness or insincerity it could be caustic also.

It was thus a life noble in its spiritual range and depth, and rich in human interests and sympathies, which after a hundred years passed through that event in the time-history of the spirit which we call death. Her life, indeed, was like the course of a river which becomes ever deeper, broader, fuller, in its flow as it draws near the sea. No wonder, then, that her son could write : " *My mother passed away in the fullness of spiritual splendour.*"

All who knew her know that their lives have been enriched by the friendship and the memory of a woman noble in face, in mind, and in soul, who helped them to realize the littleness of death, the greatness of life, and the nearness of God.

COSMO EBOR.

BISHOPSTHORPE, YORK.
October 1925.

CONTENTS

ILLUSTRATIONS

INTRODUCTORY NOTE

AMONGST my mother's papers were the Recollections of her youthful days that follow, which were written for her children and grandchildren. I have tried in Chapter II to supplement them by telling something of her later life. In the final Chapters my brother and some friends have added to this narrative by relating their personal impressions.

E. S. H.

CLOAN.

I

EARLY DAYS

THE events of nearly a century have been so numerous, and the changes so great during that time, that the record of a life which has in its course embraced this period cannot fail to possess a certain interest. Added to this, it seems reasonable that such a record may possess special interest to those immediately connected with it.

As some preface seems necessary, I will commence by an endeavour to pick up a little of our family history which might otherwise be unrecorded, and indeed totally forgotten.

My father's family was a branch of the Burdons or Bourdons of the county of Durham, of whom many traces are found, I believe, in the south-west of England,

3

and also in the middle of Scotland. They were of Norman origin.

My father, Richard Burdon, was the youngeſt son of Sir Thomas Burdon of Jesmond—originally Jesus Mount—near Newcaſtle, and he was born on March 31ſt, 1792. The ruins of a chapel remain in my recolleƈtion, and I have a hazy idea that a convent or nunnery formerly exiſted on this spot. My great-grandfather, Richard Burdon, lived to a great age, and, at the period of life when infirmities are apt to grow upon us, sat on horseback with as good a seat as could be possessed by a man of thirty years of age, and rode to hounds. When eighty years old he used to insiſt on my father following him out on a mule, and he was in the habit of riding over hedge and ditch, never allowing the child to think or say he was afraid. The result was that his namesake and grandson never knew what fear was. He had two sons by his second, and a daughter Dorothy by

his first, marriage.   I have a perfect recollection of my great-uncle Richard.   He lived
at the Shield Field, Newcastle, and had one
of the most comfortable houses one can
imagine, with a garden and field attached
to it.   It was full of old cupboards, and in
these cupboards we children aways found
something nice which he delighted to divide
amongst us, always giving my eldest brother
Richard a double portion.   The curiosities
which that house contained often come
back with vividness to my recollection—
the old chests containing pieces of old court
dresses, shoe buckles, and other relics of
olden days.

My father had three brothers, all of
whom were older than himself.   One must
have died as an infant, and another comparatively young.   William was the eldest,
and the second brother was Thomas, like
his father.   William and Thomas were both
sent to the Grammar School at Durham,
where my father followed them, after leaving

Ovingham, a preparatory school, to which he
was sent at the early age of six, and to which
he and his brother made many melancholy
journeys in a post-chaise. He used often
to speak of his experiences there. The
little boys were all called out in the morning
by Mr. Birkett, the head master of the
school, with the words, " All out to bathe,
boys." They were each one of them taken
hold of by one foot and plunged into the
Tyne without a moment's hesitation. They
became excellent swimmers in consequence.
Being the youngest pupil, my father often
had unpleasant adventures, such as being
shut up in the village hearse. At Durham
he had as schoolfellow Mr. Erskine of
Linlathen, well known in Scottish religious
history, who used, when he lived in Edinburgh, to tell me about their doings. He
possessed a perfect horror of the school
and of the system pursued there, but my
father did not have the same; indeed, he
always retained a liking for it. My father

often told us of the tricks the boys played
on Mr. Britton, the head master, but he
seldom got into disgrace himself owing to
his sense of humour and quickness. There
was a boy who used to try Dr. Britton very
much, and when he had to parse the verb
" to go," and began " *vado*, I go," had a
book thrown at his head by the doctor,
who said angrily, " And you *do* go, sir."
Mr. Britton had a good opinion of his
powers and dignity, and used to ask his
pupils, " Boys, do you know who is the
first Greek scholar Oxford has produced ? "
And then, in measured tones, he replied,
" James Britton, boys ; James Britton ! "
He was immensely offended when some
gentlemen, probably " doing " Durham,
inquired at the door whether they could
hear the boys sing. " Zing, sir ! " retorted
the Doctor, " we don't zing here ; this is
the Grammar School ! " Years afterwards
my father showed us an arm-chair which
used to be almost constantly minus one arm,

and to betray a constant tendency to lose
that member if repaired.   The reason of
this symptom in the chair was that the
Doctor sat in it while hearing lessons, and
if he sat sideways it was more possible to
get a sight of the page.   But woe to the
boy whose lesson was on the other side of
the book!   These were days of rough,
practical jokes.   Stoney Stratford Bowes of
Gibside, and of notorious memory, once
engaged a sedan chair out of which the
floor had been removed by himself, or by
his orders, and inveigled old Alderman
Cramlington of Newcastle into it.   The men
carrying it had been bribed, and allowed
him to go in front in the place of one of
them.   The alderman had silk stockings,
knee breeches, and pumps, the evening
having been a festive one.   As soon as
he was well seated, Mr. Bowes started off
through the streets, and, of course, on the
floor coming out, the chair knocked against
the old gentleman's shins, and he had to

run as fast as his legs could carry him!
This was among the most harmless of Mr.
Bowes's tricks. It seemed to be the manner
of that time to find amusement in rather a
coarse way.

My father was fortunate, after leaving
school, in being boarded with the Rev. Mr.
Manisty, afterwards Rector of Edlingham,
Northumberland, and father of one of our
distinguished judges. The reason he went
there was that there was no vacancy at
Oriel College when he left school, and his
uncle, Lord Stowell, wrote that it would do
the lad no harm to have another year of
preparation. This was about 1808. He
used to tell me that Mr. Manisty's training
was the making of him. I myself have a
very distinct recollection of Mr. Manisty
and of his wife, whose visits to my parents
were frequent. She used to travel in a
riding habit and hat, and was a very formidable person in our eyes, as our father and
mother were naturally anxious that we

2

children should behave well in her presence
and in that of her husband. Mr. Manisty
was an admirable teacher, and insisted on
his pupils doing everything accurately and
perfectly, no matter what trouble it cost
them.   At Edlingham my father acquired
the practice of early rising, and used to take
long walks on the moors armed with books,
which he gradually mastered.   He was a
very good Greek as well as Latin scholar.
Mr. Manisty was a thorough disciplinarian ;
he was of slight proportions and extremely
neat in his attire, wearing the recognized
silk stockings and small clothes belonging
to the country clergyman of that day.   He
used even to pull up my mother for the
misuse of words, which she, as an only
child unaccustomed to be corrected, rather
resented. I remember his reproving her for
using the word " litter " !   The rev. gentleman would stand aghast were he to drop
down at this day and hear the expressions
made use of by the present generation.

My father was his mother's favourite
child, and his love for her was very great.
But the time spent at home was never of
long duration, for he was always sent off
again to school. His aunt, Dorothy Burdon,
was very kind to him, and must have been
a very lovable woman. She was inspired
by the Methodist movement, and my father
used to express himself with regret for his
conduct towards a Methodist preacher who
was frequently a guest of his aunt's.

Sir Thomas Burdon, my grandfather, was
knighted for military and political and civic
services. He was Mayor of Newcastle and
Lieutenant-Colonel of a Volunteer Regiment, of which Lord Darlington was
Colonel. This regiment was raised, like
others, to deal with the expected landing
of the great Napoleon at Tynemouth—an
event which, fortunately, never took place.
My father was major in the same regiment.
After 1815 the Tyne Hussars, as they were
called, were disbanded, but my father's

regimental equipment remained carefully
preserved in a garret to which we children
in after-years had occasional access, and in
which we were sometimes shut up. The
frequent appearance at dinner parties of the
officers of a cavalry regiment quartered in
Newcastle impressed us with a military
fervour. Two young captains named
Philipps enjoyed a romp with us children;
and an officer, who was of a graver turn of
mind, used to take me on his knee and talk
to me beside the fire. I often sat by him
on a comfortable high stool covered with
my mother's work.

My grandmother, Lady Burdon, Jane
Scott, was a handsome woman, and termed
" Lively Vivacity," while her sister was
called " Sweet Sensibility "; they had two
distinguished brothers, who have left their
record in history. The elder, William (afterwards Lord Stowell), was born under
peculiar circumstances. When Prince Charlie
was expected to attack Newcastle Mrs.

Scott was let down in a basket over the town wall and was conveyed to Hepburn, where she gave birth to twins, of whom William was one and Barbara the other. This accidental circumstance was of much benefit to William, as it entitled him to a foundation which not only assisted himself but allowed him to help his brother in his future career. The two brothers were sent to Oxford after a sound grammar-school education at Newcastle under Mr. Moises, whom they never forgot. Their father chose University College for them at Oxford, and there they both set themselves to hard study. Soon after their return, John, the younger brother, startled the community by eloping with Bessie Surtees, the daughter of a prosperous wine-merchant in Newcastle. The two were in the habit of riding on horseback together, which gave them the opportunity to arrange their plans. I remember the house from which they made off; it was a commodious

mansion on the Sandhill, and Jack Scott
had a post-chaise in readiness to receive his
bride as she let herself down by sheets
from her window. The parents naturally
objected most strongly to the marriage, as
both were very young, and the young man
had nothing to support a wife. His father
to a certain degree relented, as he appears
to have settled £2,000 upon him, and added
another £1,000 in his testamentary disposi-
tion. To Lord Stowell he left about £25,000.
Lord Stowell, on his part, left a good deal
of money to my father.

Throughout the Scott family there was
evidence of a strong will. Barbara, the twin
sister of Lord Stowell, gave rather an
amusing proof of this. A suitor for her
hand was paying her a call when a visitor
was announced, and he, not wishing to be
seen, hid himself behind the door. She
forthwith sent him a decided negative to his
proposals, saying that a man who was
ashamed of her was not worthy of her hand.

Jane, my grandmother, was of a different nature, and did all in her power to smooth matters between her father and her brother John. She was the bearer of a note from the latter to his parents in which he told his story frankly. The father was at breakfast, and simply put the note into his pocket, and continued the meal, saying, " Jack has taken his own way and must keep it." Jane continued to stand by her brother in his troubles and not infrequently helped him in various ways. She was a remarkably clever woman, but her marriage was not ideal. Sir Thomas Burdon was a complete man of the world and spent his time in visits to various places, including Raby, Alnwick, and Ravensworth Castles. He was open-handed and generous, and was idolized in Newcastle owing to his liberal actions, while his wife, though attractive, was retiring and loved study. She liked to spend her time quietly with her sons at the Manor House of West Jesmond during their

vacations from school or college. She died
in May 1822, and in 1826 her husband
was about to marry again, this time to
a Miss Rutherford, and was occupied
in refurnishing the Manor House in preparation of the event, when his own death
put an end to the plan. Had I been a boy
I was to have had his name and been made
his heir. In 1826, the year after my birth,
there was a General Election held during
very hot weather, and in great excitement.
My grandfather was chairman at a large
political meeting, and someone opened a
window immediately behind him which
caused him to catch a chill, and he died
soon after. It was found that he had left
all his landed property to my father, the
eldest and only other surviving son being
provided for. The latter had apparently
displeased his father by not helping him in
his office in Newcastle and going to live in
London. Neither he nor the other brother
was studiously inclined when, like their

uncles, they were at University College, Oxford. The two sons of Lord Eldon and Lord Stowell respectively, William Scott and William Henry Scott, were under-graduates with their cousins at the same college. Both somehow missed their mark, and Lord Stowell's son, who was naturally shy, was attached to a lady whom his father, for some reason, did not wish him to marry, and he never got over the dis-appointment. He died young, and Lord Stowell was left with one daughter, who married first Mr. Townsend, and later Mr. Addington, afterwards Lord Sidmouth, who was Speaker for some years in the early part of last century. She lived to a con-siderable age, and was very kind to my mother in her early married life, as was the Dowager Marchioness of Sligo, whom Lord Stowell married secondly. But this marriage was one of convenience rather than attach-ment on either side. Lord Eldon's second son, John, had more ability; he married

3

Miss White-Ridley, but died young, leaving a son.

I shall now pass to my mother's family.

My mother was the only child of Sir James Sanderson, who originally belonged to a Yorkshire family. One of his sisters married the Rev. Henry Fisher, Chaplain to the Bishop of Calcutta. His mother lived at Elvington, not very far from York, and as the country was rather lonely she was subject to frequent alarms from burglars. She and her daughter, who were sleeping in the same room, were one night awakened by hearing a ladder being planted against the wall of the house. The mother immediately crept out of bed in her night attire, and approaching the window on her hands and knees opened it softly and waited till the robber put his head within. When fairly caught she held him there, while her daughter alarmed the household.

My mother spent some of her childhood in Yorkshire with her grandmother, or at

Elvington Rectory with Mrs. Fisher, and she said there used to be four Elizabeth Sandersons at the table, my mother and her aunt, and her mother and grandmother.[1] My mother was taught grammar, or, as it was then called, " the art of speaking and writing the English language with propriety," by Lindley Murray, the famous grammarian, who then, I believe, resided at York. She was a child who possessed much originality. She used to be shut up in the parish church, which was near the house, when other means failed to subdue her spirit. On one occasion she told us that she was so impressed by the fact that she had to contend with an evil spirit, that she went up into the pulpit to try to leave it there for the clergyman to deal with when he came to preach the following Sunday !

[1] Two were given the same name in the following generations, the surviving one of whom possesses an " Elizabeth Sanderson " coffee-pot which has belonged to several of the name.

Sir James Sanderson distinguished himself in the latter part of the eighteenth century by his fearless manner of grappling with the dangers and difficulties which attended the circulation of revolutionary principles in this country. He was a hop-merchant and banker, and was High Sheriff and twice Lord Mayor of London. His sympathies were with William Pitt, in whose society he frequently was. He represented Hastings in Parliament, and lost his life, it is said, by sending Pitt home in his carriage after a late sitting in the House of Commons and himself returning in a damp hackney coach.

Sir James died at the comparatively early age of fifty-two. He was twice married, first to a Miss Judd, and then to my grandmother, Elizabeth Skinner, who survived him. My mother was born two years before her father's death, and, disappointed in her sex, he left instructions that she was to be educated as a boy, and a very valuable library was left for her use. She was not to be taught music or any of the usual accomplishments of a young lady, but to be instructed in Latin, Greek, and other subjects considered suitable for a masculine mind. My grandmother, of course, endeavoured to carry out her husband's wishes, and carefully avoided teaching the child music. The love of music, however, as if by the rule of contrariety, was born in her, and she played almost by nature and without print or manuscript. Her early training was conducted at a Dame School at Clapham, where she was a fellow-pupil of Lord Macaulay, and, I believe, other youthful members of the Clapham sect. She afterwards went to a Miss Montier's school at Balham, which she liked very much, and generally rode backwards and forwards to it on a pony.

Lady Sanderson's father, Thomas Skinner, was also Lord Mayor of London, and during his term of office he headed a deputation to remonstrate with King George III

in regard to entering upon the war with
America.   He was a strong Liberal, an
adherent of Charles James Fox, and the
Duchess of Devonshire often visited him.
He resolutely refused any honour offered
to him, and, being very wealthy, was also
very generous, keeping open house in
Aldersgate Street, where he lived, for the
refugees during the French Revolution.
These refugees included many Abbés, such
as the Abbé Gautier, and this society was
in itself an education for his daughter.
Mrs. Skinner was a lady of considerable
spirit, and during the Lord George Gordon
Riots, when their house was marked for
destruction owing to the nature of their
foreign guests, she put on a blue silk gown
(blue being the Protestant colour), opened
the window, and addressed the mob, assuring
them of her non-Catholic propensities.   In
this she was successful.   It is difficult to
conceive how bitter the feeling was against
Catholics even in my own time.   As a child

our nursery governess told us that if the Roman Catholics gained power the streets would run with the blood of the Protestants. Similarly we were brought up in the nursery in terror of " Boney " and the French.

Sir James Sanderson, though, unlike Mr. Skinner, a Conservative in politics, was, like William Pitt, liberal in his views. He devoted his attention to separating young criminals from older offenders, and was President of Bridewell Hospital, which is one of the Corporations belonging to the City of London. In the hall of Bridewell there is a full-length portrait of Sir James Sanderson painted by Gainsborough. He was a very tall and handsome man, and paid great attention to his appearance. There was also a picture of him, now destroyed by fire, representing him as handing over money from his private bank to the Bank of England on the occasion of a sudden run upon it.

The wedding of Sir James Sanderson

and Miss Skinner took place from the
Mansion House, and after the bridal couple
started on their way they were landed in
the ditch—the coachman being perfectly
drunk—which did not seem a good begin-
ning for married life! The two had a country
residence on the south side of London at
Wandsworth Park. When the birth of
my mother was expected Lady Sanderson
started on her way to her town house in
order to have the best medical attendance.
She reached London Bridge, which was
then covered with buildings, one of which
was owned by her husband as a ware-
house and dwelling-house for one of his
employees, when she was taken ill. Thus
my mother was born within the sound of
Bow Bells, on September 30th, 1797.

Her father was buried in St. Mary Magnus
Church in the City, where there is a beautiful
mural tablet erected to his memory. Lady
Sanderson was overcome with grief on his
death, had the room in which her husband

lay hung with black, and gave away most of her jewellery, feeling that life had no longer any interest for her. She became acquainted with some Quaker ladies, who told her of how she might help the distressed, but her little daughter did not sympathize with their views, remarking tersely, when asked by one of the Friends how she liked their meetings, " Thy ways are not my ways." Amongst those Lady Sanderson came to know was Elizabeth Fry, whom she accompanied on her visits to the prisons. On one occasion she took my mother with her, and the young girl was deeply impressed by what she then saw.

At Clapham, where the mother and daughter lived after Sir James's death, some black boys were brought over from the centre of Africa largely through the efforts and at the cost of Robert Haldane, my future husband's uncle. They were to be trained as missionaries for that country, and a suitable staff was provided to do this

4

under the direction of Mr. Campbell. Unfortunately, the boys escaped from their con-
ductor and scampered across the common,
to the great delight of my mother as a child.

It was at this time that Lady Sanderson
became acquainted with the Rev. John
Newton, author, with Cowper, of the Olney
Hymns. It was while sitting on his knee
that her daughter first received her impressions of the love of God to sinners;
these she never lost.

Lady Sanderson's mind was not at rest
in regard to religious matters, and her maid
induced her to go to hear the Rev. William
Huntington, who at that time was a very
popular preacher. Not liking to drive to
the door, she went on foot, and on arrival
was so impressed that she became a devoted
member of his congregation. I believe the
Princess Amelia also attended his ministra-
tions. Some years later my mother was
sent to a fashionable school at Hendon
kept by seven sisters, the Misses Lockyer,

who were frequently called the " Seven Muses " ; when there she heard that her mother was about to marry Mr. Huntington. She was almost broken-hearted, but a little later she was taken seriously ill, and the kindness and devotion of Mr. Huntington won her heart. He died soon after, when my mother was sixteen. Mr. Huntington left his wife a cottage at Cranbrook, where Lady Sanderson was buried, since being a Dissenter she could not be buried in consecrated ground. It was called " My Lady's Cottage," and at one time was given to a former butler to live in. His mind had become somewhat unhinged through politics, and to the dismay of my parents they found he had put up a signboard on the cottage with the inscription " The Disappointed Politician."

On Lady Sanderson's marriage my mother became a ward in Chancery, and at the age of sixteen received an allowance of £400 a year, which made her in great measure independent of her mother. She was provided with her own room and a lady companion, who was not everything she ought to have been, for she endeavoured to bring about a far from desirable marriage without the sanction of her natural guardians. Lady Sanderson (for she retained that name) lived for five years after Mr. Huntington's death, and the mother and daughter took a house near Regent's Park, where they spent many happy days. It was at this time that they became acquainted with Mr. Richard Burdon, owing to his eldest brother having become engaged to a Miss Meux, the grand-daughter of one of Sir James's sisters. That engagement was, however, broken off through want of agreement about the quality of a sermon! The lady was apparently interested in theology, for she ultimately married a Mr. Benson, and became the mother of Father Benson, the well-known Cowley Father and Missioner, who was thus a distant cousin of ours.

My mother used to tell a rather amusing

story about one of her first meetings with my father. The young man was anxious to find out if the young lady was good-tempered, and while walking in the garden in winter he conducted her under the branch of a tree loaded with snow, which he deftly shook over her bonnet. It was an exceedingly pretty one of white crêpe, but she took the deed in such good part that he felt he was on sure ground in choosing her as the partner of his life. He did not realize that she was still almost a child, although possessing a dignity beyond her years. He wrote to her mother asking her leave to pay his addresses to her daughter, but received a courteous reply, pointing out the unsuitability of his proposal owing to her age.

My father was now at Oxford, having been sent to Oriel College on leaving Mr. Manisty's tuition. There he distinguished himself greatly, carrying off the prize for the Newdigate Poem in 1811 (the subject being the Parthenon) when only nineteen years of age. He took first-class honours in Classics, and he was elected a Fellow of his college in 1813, which secured him an income in commencing his studies for the Bar. His uncle, Lord Eldon, presented him with a handsome service of plate, and was, of course, much interested in his future success. In 1814 he gained the prize for the English Prose Essay,[1] the subject of which was a comparative estimate of the literature of the sixteenth and seventeenth centuries. He sent a copy to Lady Sanderson without comment.

In process of time the aspirant for her hand was allowed to call on Elizabeth Sanderson, who had now reached the age of eighteen, and her mother made no objection to the engagement, though, being a

---

[1] It was a disappointment to him that he was not allowed to read this essay on the visit of the Emperor of Russia, the King of Prussia, and the Prince Regent. It was supposed by the Provost that his voice would not be heard, and the substitute did not do it well.

ward in Chancery, the leave of the Lord Chancellor had to be obtained. This naturally was easily accomplished by his nephew, though her surname had by her father's will to be added to his. They were married by the Rev. Mr. Goode (Rev. William Romaine's successor) at St.George's, Bloomsbury, on February 7th, 1815, and both uncles, the Lord Chancellor Eldon and Sir William Scott (Lord Stowell, Judge of the Admiralty and Divorce Courts), were present at the wedding, as well as Sir Thomas Burdon, the bridegroom's father. A former lover stood on the steps of the church as she came out. This incident must have affected my father, because he alluded to it fifty years later, and only three days before he died. He was of an extremely sensitive nature, and had an almost morbid dread of giving pain to others.

As the custom then was, the mother of the bride travelled with the young couple, and they journeyed together as far as Clifton

—the bride attired in a riding habit, the usual fashion then and for a considerable time later.   My mother, being an only child, was a considerable heiress, and very attractive, besides having a clear intellect and power of influencing others. She had at the same time a strong will of her own. Mr. and Mrs. Burdon-Sanderson took a house in Montague Street, Russell Square, in order to be near Lord Eldon, who resided in Bedford Square. It was prepared and furnished for them by Lady Sanderson. The political agitation headed by Sir Francis Burdett led to serious riots, and during these riots the Chancellor asked his nephew to walk with him to the House of Lords. This they safely did, but a shot was fired at Lord Eldon, which passed through the skirt of my father's coat. At this period my father held a Commissioner-ship in Bankruptcy, and had been appointed by his uncle Secretary for Presentations, and was also endeavouring to practise at the Bar. The mother of Mrs. Burdon-Sanderson lived for a time with the young people, but then left them and settled at Tunbridge Wells, where she had as neighbour the rather unhappy Duchess of Wellington. Here she died.

The life in London was after some time interrupted in an unexpected way, and this requires some further explanation.

While at Oxford my father was a staunch adherent of the Church of England, neglecting neither feast nor fast. When he was there, there was quite a galaxy of notable men, more especially at his own college, Oriel. John Keble and he were contemporaries, and to the former he owed much in his spiritual life; the *Christian Year* was a favourite book with him long after their friendship dropped. I have heard him tell of his pleasure in reading with Keble on the cliffs near Shanklin, which they visited with Whately, and I always felt that spot was hallowed to me. The day

5

has dawned in both their lives, and have
not the shadows flown away? Whately
(Archbishop of Dublin), Hampden, Cople-
ston (Bishop of Llandaff), and many others
whose names have gone down to posterity,
were my father's associates or seniors in
college.   My father gained the Newdigate
in the year after Whately, and his successors
were Keble and Coleridge.   He had become
very much concerned about Divine things,
used to attend early services, and, indeed,
never allowed anything to stand in the
way of his presence at chapel twice a day.
He also hurt his health by fasting every
Wednesday and Friday. He was nicknamed
" the Methodist Parson " by his acquaintances, while Brandram, later on secretary
of the Bible Society, was called " the
Methodist Clerk."   Wilson, afterwards
Bishop of Calcutta, and Drummond, of
Catholic Apostolic fame, were also amongst
his friends. The Fellows of Oriel at this
time comprised Whately, Davison, Cole-

ridge, Atfield, and, later on, Keble, but
of them it was perhaps Whately who
exercised the greatest influence on my
father's mind. Shelley was also a contemporary, and though my father thoroughly
disapproved of his views, he was always
critical of the attitude of the authorities in
his regard, and, I believe, openly expressed
his opinion.

But after leaving Oxford his close study
of the Scriptures brought him to a further
point than he had so far reached ; and he
was also greatly influenced by reading the
Letters of the Rev. Mr. Romaine, which
made much clear to him that had hitherto
been obscure.

As Secretary of Presentations to his uncle
certain pertinent questions of right and
wrong came up acutely before him, and he
asked himself how could it be that the
Church which he loved as the Church of
Christ could give away livings to the highest
bidder and the care of souls into the bargain

which were precious in the sight of the Lord? In regard to the applications for livings that passed through his hands presents of different sorts were offered to his uncle, the Chancellor (often to his great indignation); and even to himself gifts came with the object of securing his goodwill.

Bringing all this to the test of Scripture, my father could not reconcile it with his conscience to hold his office, and spent many days and nights wrestling with God in prayer for light and direction. At this date Mr. Simeon was used as a great instrument of good in the University of Cambridge and influenced young men outside the university as well. My father was not one to flinch, even if the sacrifice cost him almost his life. He was devotedly attached to his uncle, and his work was congenial to him, but he felt he must give it up, cost him what it might; and he did so. The first intimation was a letter to Lord Stowell, declining an invitation for some festive occasion to

Erleigh Court, his country house, and giving his reasons.

For three days, I have been told, the Chancellor did not leave his room. Whether this were so or not, he was devoted to my father, and most generous to him. When my father had approached him regarding someone he wanted him to help, he told him that, if in his power, there was nothing living or dying that he would not do for him. The Chancellor had lost a most promising son, John Scott, to whom my father had a great resemblance, and his heart turned towards the latter in some measure to fill up the blank. And now he was to leave him. It was impossible for the uncles, both of them risen to greatness in their professions, to understand the motive, and they turned to the usual explanation given for such actions in lieu of a better—he was mad. And judging from a worldly point of view it was so. Was not Paul also judged by the world to be mad; and

was he not a fool that he might win
Christ ?

All this caused my father acute distress,
and resulted in a fever, which laid him very
low. My mother persuaded him to go to
Tunbridge Wells, and this ended in their
settling in that neighbourhood for nine
years. Their income was, of course, very
much curtailed by my father's withdrawal
from professional life, and they had to some
degree to practise economy, and lived at
a place called Mount Nevill, in a small house,
but with abundant accommodation for
horses and dogs, for which my father had a
natural and instinctive love. He had a power
over them which generally accompanies
the love of animals, and he never found a
horse which he could not manage, and, I
believe, never had an accident while driving
or riding himself. The house was a pretty
one, situated at the edge of a wood, and in
the midst of a large tract of country over
which he had the right to shoot. The

neighbouring properties were those of Lord
Abergavenny and Mrs. Streatfeild. This, I
have heard my mother say, was one of the
happiest periods of her life, and here her
elder children were born—the first son
after six years of married life.

I was born on April 9th, 1825, at Rother-
field, near Rotherhurst, and I must have
opened my eyes on one of the most beautiful
of English landscapes. The place is nine
miles south of Tunbridge Wells. At the
time of my birth the country was covered
with fresh verdure and wild flowers, and
when I was only nine days old I was said
to have come home covered with flowers,
the bright colours of which even then
seemed to give me pleasure. My parents
used to call me their sunny child, as there
was so much sunshine surrounding my birth.
This house had been lent to them by a
member of the Surtees family connected
with my father by marriage. They moved
later on for a visit to Eastbourne, as I did

not seem to thrive, and here they received
the announcement of my grandfather's
serious illness, but not in time, to their great
regret, to reach Jesmond to find him in life.

My father used to drive four brown horses
with black legs, which were much admired
in the county for pace and appearance, and
also a pair in a curricle. It was in the
latter that my sister and I travelled from
Tunbridge Wells to Northumberland when
I was fifteen or sixteen months old. It
took ten days to make the journey. We
had a pair of thoroughbreds in the carriage,
and on reaching the Manor House at Jesmond in the dark they leapt over a chain
that was hanging over the approach, without
damage. The journey was, however, too
much for one of them; the other, a very
handsome horse, lived for several years
afterwards, and was buried at Biddleston
at the foot of the Cheviot Hills. A clump
of trees was planted on the spot. My
father was very energetic and used to

ride through storm and wind and walk
miles in pouring rain when fishing without
caring in the least about it. In the early
days he used, like other young men, to
travel to and from Oxford on the outside
of the mail, despite cold and snow. His
horse, Coriander, was one the stablemen
found difficult to deal with, but it seemed to
recognize his hand at once. It was the
same with dogs; he had the power of
ruling men and animals.

My father was startled by finding the
responsibilities that my grandfather's will
had laid upon him and the changed life it
entailed. From this time onward our home
was in the North. The year we moved to
Northumberland, 1826, was very hot; har-
vest even in the North took place, I believe,
in July, and the corn was very short. I
do not, of course, remember it. My first
recollections are connected with the old
manor house at Jesmond, which was admir-
ably suited to the spot on which it was

6

built. My remembrance is very vivid of the rooms which we inhabited as children, and of the incidents of childhood. I recollect distinctly sitting for a picture to a Mr. Cazlitt, who drew children with wonderful success in pastel. I recollect even more vividly our being all shut into the cellar because of our lack of due respect to the butler, who had lived with my grandfather and travelled with him as valet and whose self-importance aggravated us. Three days twice a year were spent by him in brewing the ale of which he was very proud, and the housekeeper made currant and elderflower wine. My mother always insisted on our paying due respect to servants, though she was particular that they, too, should understand their duties. My brother and sister once revenged themselves upon the butler by taking the bung out of the barrel and letting his home-brewed ale run on to the floor, which was a malicious act deserving the punishment they got, for the participants were made to beg his pardon. I was too young to play a part in this iniquity, and Bradley (for that was the butler's name) used many a time to help me with my sums. I think this kind help was partly owing to the fact that we sat beside my mother's maid, who used to sew in the nursery, and he was attached to and finally married her. It was the custom then to teach children very early, and at three years old we were expected to learn to read. Before I was six I learned all the rules in Lindley Murray's smaller grammar by heart, the multiplication tables, French verbs, and a good deal of rhyme. When my younger brother was born, my sister and I were placed under the care of a governess, Miss Taylor, who was trained in a then famous school in Newcastle conducted by a Miss Kemp. She was a very strict disciplinarian, and we were vigorously punished when we infringed the laws of the schoolroom. She had rooms in a house adjoining that which we occupied while my father was building West Jesmond, his new house, and we went and came to and from her apartment, spending twelve hours of every day there under her supervision. The system of the day was to administer corporal punishment. We, or rather I, as my sister escaped from having had scarlet fever and being pronounced delicate, was shut up for a day at a time and fed only on bread and water. Sometimes it was in an empty room, and once in a room never opened in a so-called haunted house which my father had taken for the shooting season. I remember to this hour the sound of the closing heavy door. It was done for good, but I question whether it was good. It did me no harm, however, as far as I am aware, though I was naturally afraid of rats.

I used to have passages of the Bible to learn, or poetry, if I misbehaved. For a Sunday transgression I had to learn the 139th Psalm, and the words of that Psalm

sank deeply into my mind. I was often
kept awake by thought of the sinfulness
of my nature and with the sense that at
any moment judgment might be passed
upon me. I knew and felt that I was a
great sinner and that God was my Judge
and must condemn me. I used to try to
keep the Commandments of God, which I
learned by heart, but constantly failed, and
I was miserable. We were always at home
on Sundays, as we did not go to church,
and our father wrote two catechisms for us,
which we learned; one was on the Lord's
Prayer, the other on the general doctrines
of the Bible. I think now that both were
rather beyond us.

While with Miss Taylor our feet were
placed in the stocks during lesson time, and
we held a back board behind our backs,
being seated on narrow seats that only just
held us. The day commenced by our being
wakened by our nurses, taken by the two,
and plunged over head in a deep bath of

cold water. Our cribs were made for us
by the joiner engaged on the house, and
they were of pinewood without springs,
and had cross-bars on which we rested on
mattresses of straw. My sister and I slept
in separate cribs in one room, but when
we were sure to be undisturbed we carried
on conversation and even got out of bed.
Sometimes, however, we were discovered
and given over to condign punishment.
The rule of life was Spartan, but I do not
regret it. It was the custom in these times
for young people never to enter a room
where there were strangers or visitors
without dropping a curtsey, and they always
addressed their elders respectfully as " Sir "
or " Ma'am." Nor were we allowed to
speak till we were spoken to by our elders.

The Manor House of Jesmond was pronounced to be in a dangerous condition
owing to the undermining of the colliery,
and it was entirely rebuilt and a new foundation stone laid. This was done to the great

disappointment of my sister and myself, because our names were not placed on the stone, but only my brother's. From that time forward the fact of being merely a daughter rankled in my mind, and during my childhood, and for years afterwards, I used to feel as if I was nothing to anybody.

As a child I loved games of all kinds, and used to long to play cricket and go out spearing with the boys and to ride to hounds. But such was not then permitted, and we had practically no amusements.

My father gave up his military Commission, and devoted himself to the superintendence of the Wallsend Colliery, which he owned (after a time it was, however, closed), and to the building of his house. Each morning he started off at six o'clock. During the autumn regular visits were paid to Harrogate, where we lodged with Mrs. Emmott, in the centre of the Stray, near the old parish church, then under the charge of the Rev. Mr. Sheepshanks, whose brother

bequeathed the famous collection of pictures
to the nation.   I have very pleasant recollections of riding round the race-course
with my sister on our ponies.   The race-
course was over a common covered with
heath.   At six o'clock in the morning we
accompanied our father to drink the waters
at the Spa, walking through the fields for
upwards of a mile, which we greatly enjoyed.
It was in the neighbourhood of Harrogate
that I saw a man-trap in use, though I believe
it had been made illegal in 1827, or at least
the crocodile-teethed trap had been so.
Occasionally we spent a day with our
cousins at Stonefall, then in the occupation
of the Rev. Andrew Cheape.   He was
Vicar of Knaresborough, but lived in this
house, which he had built, and where he
made a home for his sister-in-law, Mrs.
Stevens, and her daughter, both of whom
had become very prominent in the religious
world.   The house was a remarkable one,
being like three houses in one, and it had

a special charm for us children. Mrs. Stevens had a large class of boys in Knaresborough, and also delivered lectures in a hall adjoining the church, then considered a very unusual thing to do, and one condemned by the bishop of the diocese. Besides this, she wrote a commentary on the Bible, which comprised, I believe, twenty volumes. Her daughter, Maria, conducted a school for girls, who were trained as nursery governesses, and Mr. Cheape had the schoolhouse erected in a field adjoining his residence at Stonefall. The pupils were well taught in the usual subjects as well as to be expert needle-women, but above all in religious matters. They also excelled in hymn-singing. Mrs. Cheape likewise wrote books, some of which I have, and took the management of her husband's farm. She also wrote on bees, a subject which she thoroughly understood.

The Rev. Mr. Sheepshanks of the parish church officiated at the marriage of a cousin

7

by marriage, Junie Jumbert (Mrs. Foster), to the Rev. James Manisty, son of the Dr. Manisty, Vicar of Edlingham, with whom my father boarded. We girls officiated as bridesmaids, and were dressed in grey satin pelisses over white figure muslin skirts and had pink drawn satin bonnets. It was a great occasion in our lives, though the marriage of Mrs. Foster left a great blank, for she had lived with my mother during her widowhood and taught us a good deal that was useful.

It may be interesting to hear what children wore in those long ago days. We were dressed in white cambric frocks in the morning with low necks and short sleeves and had broad blue or pink sashes tied behind. When we went out of doors we wore white spencers of cambric muslin with frills round the waist and long sleeves and collars and cuffs, the sashes being dispensed with. Drawn silk bonnets were worn with net caps covering the head and

bordered with tiny roses or baby ribbon.
The latter was very becoming, and net caps
were thought essential for cleanliness. In
winter we donned pelisses and beaver
bonnets for out-of-doors, and in the house
dresses of fine crimson merino. It was the
fashion then to have the drawers long,
showing the double-worked frills below the
hem of the dress. When King George IV
died in 1830 I remember the pride we had
in our black and white gingham frocks
which we wore in mourning.

Visits were sometimes paid to Rothbury
for the sake of the fishing on the Coquet,
and these we always enjoyed. We took
long rides on the hills watching the goats
which browsed on the short grass, and the
goats' milk was considered good for us.
What is now the most beautiful estate of
Cragside, the property of Lord Armstrong,
and covered with rhododendrons, azaleas,
and lithospermum, was then a rocky emin-
ence. The brilliancy of the colour as I

saw it in recent years is impossible to forget.
I have a very vivid recollection of what was
called the Thrum, the place where the
Coquet runs in a very narrow channel over
which an athletic person could leap, though
to a child it seemed full of danger. Dr.
Manisty's house was near, which was an
attraction to my parents. We also went to
live for a time at Overacres, a house situated
between Otterburn and Elsdon. There was
a considerable amount of shooting attached
to the place, which, as it was contiguous to my
father's property, suited his sporting proclivi-
ties as well as those of his friends. At this
place my mother undertook our education
instead of Miss Taylor, to our great delight.
She drew maps of different countries and
taught us about the mountains and towns
instead of merely their names, and was also
a good French scholar, through her associa-
tion with Mlle Jumbert (Mrs. Foster), of
whom I spoke.

In 1832 cholera visited the British Isles,

and being an unknown disease it perplexed the medical faculty. There was a case in a farm-house adjoining Overacres, which my mother took under her supervision. We children were given port wine daily to strengthen our systems against an attack, a treatment to which we did not object. In those days children were always given a mug of ale at dinner-time. The year was also memorable for the excitement preceding the passing of the Reform Bill. I remember the burst of feeling caused by the passing of the Bill. The news came by the Chevy Chase coach which ran between Newcastle and Edinburgh. The coach passed our own gate and at the foot of the avenue leading to Overacres the horn blew as it stopped to give it. People collected at the gate to hear the wonderful news, and, as we were fortunately without a governess at the time, I was present, though only a child of seven.

The cousins near Harrogate advised my mother (who was expecting an addition to her family) to engage a lady named Miss Forster, who had been governess to their nieces who had been sent home from India, as governess to us. The lady had been brought under the extreme evangelical influences through the Mrs. Stevens I spoke of, and her niece, Mrs. Carus Wilson, who organized a school which has been immortalized by Charlotte Brontë in *Jane Eyre*.

It was a time of strictness in the bringing up of children which was carried to a degree of severity, especially in the Yorkshire schools. I have known my boy cousin return from school black and blue from bruises inflicted by the cane, while a schoolfellow lived for three days in a chimney hiding in fear of his master's treatment. The girl cousin was punished by being locked up for days in a barn and fed on bread and water, only taken into one of the maids' rooms at night. It drove her into a spirit of resolute rebellion, while she might have been guided by kindness. But this was just a small example of what was constantly going on. We can hardly be thankful enough to Charles Dickens and Charlotte Brontë for exposing these evils.

The girl cousin I speak of, Gertrude Sandham, married a Dr. Heathcote, and they were victims of the massacre of Cawnpore. She and her husband and one of her children were among those who came down the river in the boats and were decoyed into Cawnpore under false pretences by Nana Sahib. She showed her strength of character by refusing to leave her husband, and was hacked to pieces with him and her child before being thrown down the well. Possibly her severe early training was useful to her in the terrible times she had to pass through.

My mother was very ill after her confinement, and our governess was much with her, being an excellent nurse. This left us a good deal to the care of a nursery governess (also provided by Mrs. Stevens), in whom

my mother placed the greatest confidence.
She was a perfect hypocrite, and neglected
her charges while she amused herself. She
was in the habit of singing hymns and
putting on a sanctimonious face before her
employers.

A sister of this nursery governess was
engaged by my mother to teach the children
of the pitmen who worked in my father's
colliery. She was well qualified for her
work. The school was held in the village
of Brandling Place. The hair of a little
girl had caught fire on one occasion, and
my mother engaged a hairdresser to cut off
all the long curls which were then worn
by girls. Such high-handed treatment
would not now be tolerated! In those
days the line of demarcation between classes
was very strong. But though our hearts
were touched by hearing of the boys who
were sent up chimneys to sweep them and
who often stuck fast with disastrous results,
and of those who were laid hold of and

made to serve aboard ship, in our neighbourhood conditions were fairly good.

In 1833–4 we had a very happy time at
Biddleston, a house which my father hired
from the Selbys while his own was being
built, in spite of the attempted influence of
our nursery governess.   My happiness was
only marred by the thought of my own
sinfulness, which never left me.   In the
morning we sat in our mother's boudoir.
We read through Voltaire's *History of Louis
XIV*, *Charles XII*, and *Peter the Great*,
and looked up words which we could not
translate.   We were also greatly interested
in the intrusions of the housekeeper and
coachman who came for their daily orders.
My father then rented about 10,000 acres
of shooting, and my mother had a large
household to provide for, besides arranging
for the outside establishment of ten horses
and ponies and about forty dogs.   Being
out of the range of shops, there were six
oxen and twenty sheep slaughtered during

8

the year to supply the wants of the establishment. One of the oxen was killed at
Christmas, and divided into joints for
distribution among the people in the village.
During the time we were at Biddleston
scarlet fever broke out, and my mother was
constant in her attendance on the sick,
carrying out the doctor's instructions. She
used to keep a special dress for these visits,
which she laid aside immediately on her
return home. My mother always kept a
considerable supply of medicine, and never
travelled without a large medicine chest in
the carriage : rather cumbersome luggage.

My father was an active member of the
magisterial bench at this time. On one
occasion he was alone with his son on the
moors when he was surrounded by several
poachers, among whom were some whom
he had had occasion to sentence as Justice
of the Peace. One of these threatened to
shoot him. He sat down quietly among
them, sending his son on his pony for

A PORTRAIT OF HER FATHER, RICHARD BURDON SANDERSON
Painted by my Mother.

assistance if necessary. After entering into conversation with them he handed them his gun, which he told them was one of Manton's best, and a very valuable one, showing them by this that he had confidence in them. They were all much gratified with this, and their interview ended in their telling him that he was the pluckiest gentleman they had ever met and promising never to disturb his game, which promise they faithfully kept.

I think my descendants would like to know what my parents were like and how they dressed. My father was very upright in bearing and his clothes always fitted him. He had a distinguished appearance. His hair was dark brown and he had full grey eyes. He was athletic and had a well-proportioned figure, a very neat leg and ankle and a good foot, so that he both walked and danced well, as well as being a good oarsman and pugilist. He was always very carefully dressed, and used to wear bands of whalebone like stays. I think this was helpful to him in hunting, besides which it was the fashion with gentlemen in those days. When I first remember him he wore small clothes and silk stockings when in evening dress and a white waistcoat such as has now come into fashion again. My mother also was decidedly handsome. She held herself well and gave an impression of command by her person and speech. She was also very upright and very carefully dressed. Her gowns were short enough to show the sandalled satin shoes and silk stockings about which she was very particular. The gowns had very little waist, and a gold band reaching very high up on the figure. The sleeves of the gown were very short, but she wore tulle or fine net reaching to the wrists, around which she wore rather heavy bracelets. Her light-brown hair was dressed in bows very high, and she had a great quantity of it. This was surmounted by a large (what would now be called) " picture hat," with an overhanging ostrich plume. The hat was of blue or white satin such as was then worn in the evening. She had a natural love of gaiety and dancing, though her manner of life changed entirely when she became set on spiritual things. My father and mother never crossed their letters as was done so much in later days, and their missives were carefully folded and sealed. Even when penny postage was introduced and sealing letters ceased to be necessary, they were always carefully written and addressed. Nowadays letters are for the most part telegraphic communications. My father occasionally smoked, but only in the open air when riding or walking. He would not have thought of doing so indoors.

In 1835 the house at Jesmond was ready for occupation, and shortly afterwards the cousins I have spoken of came to visit us and share our lessons with Miss Forster. We usually moved to Otterburn Dene for

the spring and summer. My father and
mother never separated as a rule, and it
was quite an event when he left her for four
days to see after his sporting establishment
in the hills. This was their only separation
during their married life of nearly fifty years.

If it had not been for the atmosphere
of introspective religion I should have
enjoyed my life, but Miss Forster's residence with such powerfully-minded women
as Mrs. Stevens and Mrs. Cheape had
drawn her into their vortex. Personal influence which is excited by a subtle power
over the mind is, I think, evil, especially
when based on religious grounds. Religion
has too often been the wedge of torture,
and to sensitive natures an engine of cruelty.
One is thankful that the days have passed
when such despotism is excited in the name
of religion. I shudder at it and rejoice to
see our boys and girls brought up in the
light of day with the full glare of public
opinion blazing on the work of their educa-

tion. It is their own fault if they are not
independent thinkers. My own life was at
this period saddened by the Jesuitical
system quite unknown to either parent.
At one time tales told by the hypocritical
maid spoken of before quite changed my
mother's attitude to me, which pained me
very much, and we were too proud to tell
tales on the servant as we might have done.
We were watched continually and our
actions and words and thoughts construed
into meanings of which we never dreamt.
Prayers were directed *at* us by our governess.
She had real kindness, and her manners
charmed most people, but it was the system
that was wrong.

The shooting lodge in which we lived so
much—Otterburn Dene—is situated in the
midst of moorland, and as there is only
one road to it we had to go round a long
way or ride over the moor. Medical attendance was difficult, and the administration of
leeches was considered an excellent remedy

for many diseases. The country doctor had a very large district in which to practise. He appeared in my room attired in a bright green coat with brilliant brass buttons, corduroy trousers, and top-boots, a stout riding-whip in his hand. I was then suffering from a sharp attack of rheumatism, and he bled me successfully after one or two unsuccessful attempts owing to the failure of his instrument. I remember his asking me, " Wud ye like to be bluided ? " which I answered in the affirmative, as I was thankful for any proposal of relief. He accordingly proceeded, asking in the first place for list, which he explained was " the stuff ye make garters of," and this he rolled firmly round my arm. After the first unsuccessful effort he remarked, " I see the artery ; we must be careful." He took a basin full of blood and stopped the bleeding by folds of lint with some difficulty. I felt relieved, but very exhausted. I was about fourteen at the time, and the illness was

produced by my bathing with my sister at
Otterburn Dene at Christmas time in the
open air in a bath which had been made
in the grounds, after having the ice,
which was of considerable thickness, broken
by sledge-hammers. It was not a wise pro-
ceeding, though it amused us, and resulted
in rheumatism. That winter was very
severe, and the water in our bedroom used
to be frozen in the morning. It was not
then considered the proper thing for young
people to use hot water in their ablutions,
and there were very few fixed baths in those
days. There was one at Jesmond in a
remote part of the top of the house, but it
was not constantly used.

On the few occasions when we were free
from nurse or preceptress we had a sunny,
happy time walking on the moors and
watching the lambs. We would go forth
on our ponies under the old coachman's
care, fording the streams and climbing the
sides of those green hills which, I think, are

nowhere so beautiful as on the Cheviot
range. Sometimes my mother wanted to
drive herself, but that did not afford us the
same amusement as riding did. We had,
generally speaking, to sit outside when she
made visits and wait, which at no time is a
very lively position, but the conversation
of the coachman and groom, who were
intelligent men, entertained us. In early
days at Jesmond my mother drove four
white ponies, two of which were of Arab
breed. The coachman once tried to drive
six, but when harnessed they refused to
move from the door! The coachman,
James Lithgow, was even a greater Tory
than his master, my grandfather. He used
to carry a white silk embroidered flag at
election time with "Liddell for ever"
floating from the back of the carriage.
The barouche was claret-coloured, as were
the livery and saddle cloths, mounted in
silver. The rosettes on the ponies' heads
were crimson, as were the small clothes of

the men. We children rode a great deal
with the coachman, and he occasionally
went into a public-house called " The Leg
of Mutton " to get a glass of beer. Our
delight was to elude him and get out of
sight ! He eventually took somewhat to
the bottle, and my mother, though sorry to
dispense with him after thirty-five years'
service, distrusted his driving after some
anxious experiences, so that when my father
gave up the hounds in 1837 the huntsman
became coachman. In the North my mother's
calls were few and far between, as we had
no near neighbours. My brother went
with my father when he was shooting, and
often brought home game on his pony in
the saddle bags. When alone with our
parents we were perfectly happy ; but that
was seldom.

In those days it was not unusual to drive
six-in-hand. The Duke of Northumberland
travelled from Alnwick to London in the
manner of a royal progress. The carriages

and plate were, of course, conveyed by road, and at that time only white and grey horses were used. Horses were ordered some time before at the Turk's Head, Newcastle, and there were thirty at least in requisition. All noblemen, as a rule, travelled with four horses, as did a good many commoners as well. Times have changed since then, and certainly for the better. There was a strong dividing-line between the upper and lower classes, so called, and it was the aim of the latter to curry favour with the others. Appointments were procured by favour, and everyone strove to bring influence to bear on his own or friends' behalf. The Reform Bill did a great deal to break down these barriers, but, I think, almost as much, the railways.

The first locomotive was a curious grass-hopper-looking machine that made a tre-mendous noise, and if our ponies came anywhere near it they at once made off in terror. At the time of which I am writing

Lord Armstrong (as he afterwards became), Mr. Grainger, and Mr. Stephenson were making their mark in the world. The last-named my father knew well, and he did all he could to encourage him. The future Lord Armstrong used to pass through my father's grounds on his way to his work. I remember seeing Mr. Hudson, the railway king, at Carlisle. He had begun life as a stable-boy and was never properly educated, but he had a mathematical head. Many amusing stories were told of his wife, who was taken up by the Duchess of Leeds, who ran her parties. When buying a pair of globes she was shown the terrestrial and celestial globes, and said, " Oh no, I want the pair to match ! " Hudson lost his money through speculation, his fine friends left him, and on his desk were found these words : " Riches take wings and fly away."

My mother drove us to see the first balloon ascend, and we were greatly excited at the event. I was also much impressed by seeing the treadmill of the Newcastle prison; it seemed a barbarous form of punishment.

The pitmen in the part I knew were mainly Methodists, and there were schools in most of the villages, a green for playing quoits, a general bakery, and wash-house. On the whole, they were of a moral and upright class, with comfortable, well-built houses in which they took great pride. An eight-day clock and well-polished chest and other furniture were kept scrupulously clean and bright by the wives and daughters. They mostly contrived to have small bits of garden. There was thus little, if any, poverty there, though there were wandering beggars. I remember one of these who was selling soap the quality of which he extolled. The cake purchased at the back door was indeed valuable, for it contained his treasury very well plenished, which had accidentally found its way into the wrong place!

I was always very fond of flowers, and the wild flowers of the moors gave me much pleasure, as did collecting pebbles and fossils. Our gardener, who accompanied my parents from Sussex, was an exceptionally intelligent man, and when tulips were first introduced he cultivated them successfully, as he also did other flowers, such as double stocks, then considered rare.

The fair at Elsdon, a village near us in the north of Northumberland, was held in the autumn, and we were taken to see it as a great treat. I recollect the village vividly, situated as it is round a green with a rising ground where is the castle and below that the church. In front of the latter there were at this time placed the stocks, in which were put the feet of drunken and disorderly people. I have a perfect remembrance of seeing men lying in them. They lay on their backs with their feet a little raised, but held fast by the ankles so that they could not move. Whoever was placed in the stocks was a legitimate subject for the taunts and jeers of the villagers, who scrupled not to make

use of the opportunity afforded. I have
not infrequently thought that it was a fit
and proper punishment for those who made
themselves a torment to their neighbours !

At the fair there used to be stalls for
gingerbread, which seemed to us better
than any other gingerbread we ever tasted.
On one occasion when our mother was visiting Archdeacon Singleton's sister, who lived
at the castle, the Duke of Northumberland
came out and spoke to us while we were
waiting in the carriage at the door. I
remember that he wore a soft cap on his
head, which we children thought strange for
a duke ! Mrs. Singleton was a woman of
keen intellect and discernment, and she read
a great deal. Ladies of her type are becoming more rare as education levels all ranks,
but while they lived they exercised no small
influence on society. Colleges and schools
have altered the complexion of society, and
the old-fashioned delicate polish of woman-
hood is lost, though for utilitarian purposes

the education is excellent. My mother belonged entirely to the old school. She was
gifted beyond moſt women, and was entirely
in her element with ladies like Mrs. Singleton.

I only once saw my great-uncle, Lord
Eldon, and that was on the occasion of
one of our visits to Harrogate. We reſted
at Rushyford, and he had a small property
there called Eldon, from which he took his
title. The inn at Rushyford was an excellent one with a capital garden. It ſtood by
itself in the London Road, and was in
those days full of travellers. As we drove
along we ſtopped to pick marsh-mallows and
honeysuckle and other flowers, which was
a delight to me.

The winter of 1836 was remarkable for a
heavy fall of snow, and it was necessary to
leave the moorland home for Jesmond. The
great difficulty was to reach the highway
from Edinburgh to Newcaſtle through two
miles of unfinished road. The heavy
travelling carriage was with difficulty dragged

10

along by two pairs of horses. A stream
had likewise to be crossed which, though
covered with ice, gave no foothold to the
horses.

The year 1837 was an eventful one in a
certain sense, for in the autumn of the year
a stranger appeared unexpectedly at our
house on the moors. He had travelled all
the way from Clifton to see my father, and
he remarked on arrival that he had been
greeted by " the unholy sound of dogs."
This came from my father's pack of harriers !
The visitor, who was the Hon. Paul
Methuen, thought this a strange thing as
coming from the house of a Christian man,
and very nearly turned back. He was a
Plymouth Brother, so called. He and my
father spent much time together during his
visit studying the Scriptures, and he persuaded my father to adopt his views regarding baptism, and before he left he baptized
my father by immersion. Like the experience
of the eunuch in the evangelist Philip's

case, he then departed to the south, and they never met again.

The argument used in favour of adult baptism and the account of the baptism of Our Lord Himself impressed his family also, and my sister and myself also were baptized for the second time. This event brought a great joy into my life that had been so troubled before, and a new sense of the presence of God.

My father now retired much into a contemplative life, busying himself with writing and reading. Our lives hence went on in an even flow, studying French, Italian, and German with our governess and masters when they could be got. In the afternoons we read history aloud, and were questioned upon it. In this way we studied the histories of Hume, Smollett, Russell, Buchanan, Rollin, and Crevier, besides Mitford's *Greece* and other similar books. In the evening my father read to us *Paradise Lost*, Cowper's *Task*, Dryden's works, and Pope's *Homer*.

With our Italian master we read Tasso and
Metastasio.   We often made long excursions
riding and walking.

In 1838 there was another severe winter,
of which there were several just then.   The
Thames was frozen over and tents erected
upon it.   Early in January Lord Eldon died
at the advanced age of eighty-eight.   My
parents went to London for this winter, and
we were left in the care of our governess.   I
have a very dreary impression of this period ;
the days seemed so intensely dull and long.
Letters came but seldom, as postage was
considerably over one shilling.   I remember
the intensity of the cold when we drove
fifteen miles to visit a dentist named Nightin-
gale who came to the inn at Cambo.   I
drove with Miss Forster in an open dog-
cart over the bleak moor in a snowstorm.
Not far from the roadside on a gibbet was
hung the effigy of a tramp called Winter,
who murdered an old woman in sight of
that place.   The murderer was discovered

by a boy, who was unusually observant, through his footprints, and afterwards he was condemned to death and hung in chains.

In the north of Northumberland there were frequently no proper roads, merely cart tracks, and it was customary for the farmer and his wife to ride together on horseback in pillion fashion, she holding tightly by her arms round her husband's waist. In this manner they went to church. The population of Otterburn was mainly Presbyterian, the few landed proprietors being the sole representatives of the Established Church. Amongst the Presbyterians were the New and Old Lights, so called. There was a great struggle to get a site for a church and small manse, and my father exerted himself in assisting the body to get this. There was a Mrs. Waddell, a very clever woman, who did much for the community, in which she was a leader. The Waddells had a successful woollen manufactory, which is still carried on.

A custom which has ceased was that of giving mourning rings to the relatives and special friends of those who died, and also of giving black silk to the clergyman who officiated at the funeral. The silk was most useful to the clergyman's wife !

This was a time of great public disturbance and distress in England and Ireland. As regards ecclesiastical affairs my father considered that the High Church movement was likely to lead the Church of England into the clutches of Rome, and his fervent desire was to see her free and separated from the State. The Church of England was at this time in a very dead state. The Oxford Movement troubled the waters and has borne forth fruit since then.

In 1839 I fell ill, and my parents thought a journey to Edinburgh would be beneficial. We travelled there in a travelling chariot with post-horses, but found that the hotel to which we were recommended (Manuel's, in St. Andrew Square) was full, so that we

went to lodgings near. The day on which
we arrived was, unfortunately, found to be
a faſt day, and in those times this day was
ſtrictly observed and no food was to be
procured but by begging and borrowing.
At length, to our relief, for we were very
tired and hungry, some was obtained. At
that time sedan chairs were ſtill in use.
Things were very simple; a serving-maid
went without shoes and ſtockings even in
what were considered good lodgings. I
remember our arrival at Fushie Bridge Inn
on our way to Edinburgh, and our being
attacked by the supposed original of Walter
Scott's Meg Dods, who was not sparing in
the assaults of her tongue. We had some
dispute about the poſt-horses she supplied,
which were none of the beſt. She also
gave us in forcible language a far from
favourable character of the wife of one of
the neighbouring lairds. In Edinburgh I
was intereſted in visiting the Zoological
Gardens, which had a good collection of

animals, but it was situated near Bellevue Crescent and exposed to north and east winds. I was glad when the animals were removed.

The year 1840 was also one of which I have no pleasant memory. I never felt quite well, and we went on drearily with our studies, the only bright intervals being those spent with our parents. In 1841 it was much the same. My father was engaged in writing and publishing pamphlets, and my mother helped him, so that they were absorbed in their work. We had masters when we were residing in Newcastle, but otherwise were entirely under the care of our governess. When our parents became more exclusively religious and devoted to religious efforts, excellent in themselves, it withdrew them much from the society of their children. For many years I was delicate and required care, and this prevented my accompanying my brothers, as did my sister. I had a succession of ailments and

illnesses, some of them childish, which I
had escaped hitherto owing to our quiet
life, but pleurisy and jaundice were included;
and I was more or less of an invalid, although
seldom confined to my room. I had also
constant headaches owing to a fall on my
head from a spring cart. We found our lives
decidedly dull and flat, as our governess was
not one who gave us any incentive to learn.
My parents, fortunately, thought I had a
talent for drawing, and I was put under the
direction of Mr. Perley Parker, an artist of
considerable reputation in Newcastle. I
enjoyed these lessons immensely and worked
with a will. My father took a keen interest
in all I did, which helped me greatly. I
used to work beside him when he read,
and it was then that I began a fire-screen
with my father's arms, which I set aside,
but completed in 1901. My father was an
excellent reader having been taught by
Mrs. Siddons.

Later on he became deeply interested

11

in the movement in the Church of Scotland called the Disruption, and helped it in every way he could. Dr. Candlish, Dr. Guthrie, and others of the leaders were his guests in Northumberland, and I well remember the torrent of eloquence that proceeded from Dr. Candlish when he gave an address during his visit to Newcastle. This and other matters tended to bring my father out of the extreme retirement in which for some years he had lived, and we taught in a Sunday School held in a chapel which my father purchased and in which he spoke; my sister, who was musical, trained the children in singing during the week. I had not the physical energy to do very much. Weakness of body is apt to lead to a condition of mind that makes all our surroundings look dark.

LATER LIFE
TOLD BY HER DAUGHTER

II

LATER LIFE

So far the records left by my mother have been of her childhood. It may be left to me to give a short account of her subsequent life, in regard to which there are a considerable number of notes in her handwriting.

From what she herself tells, it may be judged that her early life was far from a happy time, though it was interspersed with affectionate recollections on which she loved to dwell. She was a true Northumbrian and was never tired of pointing out the virtues of her fellow-countrymen. The physical aspect of the country appealed to her as no other did, and to the end of her life nothing gave her more pleasure than to talk of the moors and rivers she loved so well.

The tragedy was that the child's life should be so clouded by the influence of a mistaken view of what religion meant. She often said that she used to wonder why it was a crime to be a child. She was naturally full of fun and mischief, and frequently told us how her sister and she tried to conceal the results of their childish misdeeds, which sometimes involved a bleeding nose! But she was also extremely sensitive, and what her sister took in a matter-of-fact way, and not too seriously, to her meant acute pain. This explains nights of weeping over imaginary sins and despair about her hopes of salvation. With her own children she had the utmost dread of dealing with religious things in a personal way or of encouraging them to express themselves in an unnatural fashion.

Much was due to the influence of the governess, but our grandmother was a woman of great force of character who wished her children to be perfection and

MY MOTHER'S EARLY HOME AT JESMOND, NORTHUMBERLAND.

CLOAN, THE HOME OF LATER DAYS.
From a Sketch by Herself.

who was too apt to believe those in whose care she had placed her daughters rather than themselves. When our mother was still in the schoolroom the governess made up her mind that her pupil had schemed to elope by a window with a clergyman who was her brother's tutor. This was an absolute fabrication, but the young man, half-amused, half-indignant at being told that he might not shake hands with the girls, shot a heron, and using its long bill, held it out, saying, " Surely we may shake hands with this ! " The result, however, was disastrous, for our mother was dispatched in disgrace to the seaside with her governess. She was too proud to protest that if she had been going to elope she would have gone by the front door, not by a window ! But the matter hurt her deeply.

The succeeding years were years of ill-health, and the uneventful life may have tended to accentuate the delicacy. There was a scheme to send the girl to London,

there to work at Sass's famous studio under
the chaperonage of an old friend. She had
real artistic gifts, and the plan was delightful to her, but, alas, it was condemned as
unsuitable before it matured! The only
alternative, therefore, was to continue her
painting as best she could at home.

About the age of twenty-one, after a
severe illness, our mother was sent to the
South to recruit, accompanied by a brother
—the younger brother to whom she had
taught his letters, and who, as Sir John
Burdon-Sanderson, of Oxford, was to become famous as a physiologist. A long visit
to old and valued friends in London was a
source of great delight to the country-bred
girl. She saw the sights of London, including her father's rooms at Lincoln's Inn,
as well as the kitchen at the Reform Club,
where the famous Soyer was at work on the
cutlets of the day. In those times no young
girl could go out to walk without an escort,
or a manservant behind her, and to enter

an omnibus was beyond the pale unless a
gentleman were on either side. But, as
was likely, a young man paid his addresses
to her, and, indeed, fell passionately in love
with her. He was, our mother used to say,
one of the most attractive men she ever met,
and the interests of the two were alike so
far as art and literature were concerned,
besides which he was full of the love of
adventure such as was sure to appeal to a
courageous and high-spirited girl. In fact,
there would appear to have been no hindrance to an alliance which on a worldly side
would have been advantageous. There was,
however, one drawback, and that a very
serious one. The young man was morally
correct in every way, but he was not religious
in the view of our grandparents, and our
mother herself did not feel sure of his being
a Child of God.

It was a bitter trial that our mother
passed through when she rejected her lover,
and one that left an effect upon her all

12

through her long life.   Her father, being
evidently conscious of what might befall
her on leaving her quiet home and entering
the world, had given her a sentence from one
of the Puritan divines before leaving which
influenced her greatly. These are the words :
" Take Christ for your Husband and He
will provide one to His own liking.   Do
nothing without consultation, the Word
of God and prayer.   God bless you, my
dear child."

Her mental condition was afterwards
very much upset, despite her father's constant assurance that she had acted rightly
in the sight of God, and the following year
likewise was one of severe illness, diagnosed
as heart disease, during which her life was
despaired of. Convalescence was very slow.
A journey to the seaside at Newbiggin did
much good, but even more, perhaps, the
relief from constant application of leeches
and other medical treatment. A wise friend
recommended riding and open air instead

of constant confinement indoors, and nature accomplished what medical art had failed to perform.

After this the younger brother went to study medicine in Edinburgh somewhat against the wishes of the parents, and the elder brother married. So that gradually the extraordinary isolation in which the young people had lived was being relieved. As our mother herself says in her notes, it could not possibly have been wise to separate the young people so entirely from those of their own ages or station in life. It was a singular experience, as she remarks, and might, but for their deeply religious training, have had disastrous effects. In some ways it may have strengthened their characters and made them independent of outside influences and amusements, but it was also calculated to make them morbid. Their own good sense alone prevented this from happening. The girls had always longed to go to school, but our grandfather had a

horror of schools, especially for girls. As
he said in writing of this : " Modesty was
to be their highest accomplishment, and the
worst attainment was that flippancy and
forwardness that too often distinguish pro-
ficients in these schools of modern inven-
tion." His own daughters were certainly
free from such vices, though the cost might
have been high.

The years 1848–50 were turning-points
in the history of our country, and also in
our mother's family life, for three or four
very happy years were then spent in
Devonshire, whither her parents had
moved to escape the rigours of a northern
climate.

Once more my mother was ill, this time
with scarlet fever, and that delayed the
journey of the two girls to join their parents.
The silver-chest and her sister's harp were to
travel with them, and it often amused us to
hear about the dread inspired by the journey,
which (though by this time was to be made by

rain) involved many changes and consequent anxieties. But for the excellence of their manservant it would hardly have been successfully accomplished. And she spoke of the relief of seeing their parents' old family chariot and postilion meeting them, probably at Exeter.

They settled in a very pleasant house about five miles from Plymouth called Belle Vue, belonging to a Mr. Bulteel. My grandfather had a special friend in the Rev. James Harris, a clergyman who had left the Church of England and become what was known as a Plymouth Brother; and amongst the various families of Harris and Bulteel and Legh Richmond, a good deal intermarried, there were many agreeable acquaintances in the neighbouring district, while there were other friends like the Derrys in town. The village people were equally friendly, and there was occupation for the girls in visiting these and looking after the children who came to the Sunday

School. The girls walked and drove in the
Devonshire lanes, but, above all, made
friends, and our grandfather was alarmed
by the cards of invitation that poured in to
a new and attractive family in the county.
Of course the society was still religious;
our mother was known in Plymouth as
the "handsome Methodist," and the rule
of life was very strict. But the agreeable
company, combined with the soft air, gave
her new life.

Our grandfather held services in a loft
or granary attached to the house, and in
these he was assisted by Mr. Harris and Mr.
Bulteel. It was found that education in the
day school (a church school) was miserable,
and my grandmother procured a good
teacher from Scotland and opened a day
school for the children. Their ignorance
astonished their teachers, but they were
quick and responsive and appreciative of
their instructors. My mother used to tell
her surprise on asking one child to repeat a

hymn, when she recited the rhyme which begins :

Matthew, Mark, Luke, John,
Bless the bed that I lie on.

In the country houses round there were excellent collections of pictures, and my mother copied a picture of Mrs. Bulteel of Belle Vue for her son-in-law, Captain Harris, who, being artistic, helped her greatly in her work. Another neighbour, Lady Cal-mady, a pupil of Lawrence, also encouraged my mother ; she possessed some very good examples of Lawrence's work. Other friends were the Rundles at Tavistock. Mr. Rundle, a banker there, was Liberal Member for Tavistock in the days when the Duke of Bedford controlled the representation of the burgh, and, besides being Liberal in politics, the family belonged to the Evan-gelical section of the Church of England. My mother formed a close friendship with the only daughter, who later became Mrs. Charles and wrote *The Schönberg-Cotta*

Family and many other well-known books. This friendship lasted till Mrs. Charles's death. There was a pleasant society at the Rundle home, largely composed of Liberal politicians and those concerned in the Repeal of the Corn Laws.

The younger brother was now in Paris and present during the *coup d'état*, when he saw, what was not realized for long, the bloodshed that then occurred. After a time our mother's two sisters went to study music and painting there, leaving her at home with her parents.

It is not to be supposed that she had been without aspirants for her hand in this pleasant Devonshire circle, but her heart was in no way touched, and until the visit of our father to Plymouth she had always decided to remain single. He had come to see his sister, the wife of a retired general, who had fought in the Sikh War, and who was resident near Plymouth. Our father had been a widower

for two or three years and had a family
of young children. He was the son of
James Haldane, in former days her father's
most valued friend, who had died not long
before. In November 1852 our grandfather
announced to his daughter our father's
wishes, after the manner of the time, and
though my mother at first put the matter
aside, at his request she gave the suppliant
a personal interview. He was a determined
suitor, and kept up a correspondence which
breathed a spiritual atmosphere that gradually inspired her with the conviction that
this and no other was the path opened up
to her, and that it was her mission to care
for the motherless children. Our grandfather
was sympathetic, as on the religious side all
was well, but our grandmother was more
than dubious, considering that five young
children created a formidable barrier. Also
she had different plans for her daughter,
which strengthened her feelings. The end
was that my mother refused to consent to

the marriage until her own mother con-
sented to attend it, and this delayed matters
for the best part of a year.

Our parents were married on July 27th,
1853, at Plymstock, by the Rev. James
Harris and the Rev. Bellenden Bulteel, and
her way to the chapel—a distance of a
mile—was strewn with flowers by the
Sunday scholars and village friends. There
were many kindly faces smiling at the
bride, who was attired in a beautiful silver-
grey moiré silk gown with a Honiton lace
cape and a veil of the same. It was supposed
that one who married a widower should
wear grey. Her bonnet for going away
was of chip with ostrich plumes. After the
ceremony a tear fell from the dear father's
eye, which he quickly removed, and she
used to say that this almost upset her, as it
was a thing she had never seen before. Her
devotion to her father and his to her were
constant and deep.

The first part of the honeymoon was

spent in the Isle of Wight, where the bride and bridegroom visited the grave of "The Dairyman's Daughter," the subject of a well-known story written by Mr. James Harris's father-in-law, the Rev. Legh Richmond. Subsequently they went to Paris, and our mother often spoke of the brightness and beauty of Paris in those days and of the attractive appearance of the Empress Eugénie, then a beautiful young woman.

On returning to Scotland a new life opened up for my mother. She was fortunately met by the entire love of the children for whom she had undertaken to be a mother and for whom through life she retained a deep affection—an affection which was fully reciprocated by themselves and, later on, by their families. The mother of our father's first wife, Mrs. Makgill of Kemback, a very handsome and charming woman, was also most helpful, and so were others of her family.

I remember so well her account of the

change in atmosphere between Devonshire and Scotland, and the certain forcible and characteristic but rather narrow relatives who came into her life and for a time were undoubtedly trying to her, though in themselves they were well-meaning and active in good works. My mother's wish was to help those who had fallen by the way, especially the younger women who had gone astray ; and this she did by simple personal talk and appeal, as she never cared for organizations in themselves. But in those days the more austere religion reigned, and there was a limit beyond which a young married woman might not go. Particularly was she condemned for exerting herself in regard to a poor woman condemned to death for killing, in a fit of passion, the paramour of her husband. My mother at the time was expecting an infant, and the woman had infants of her own and the case appealed deeply to her.

I think it was partly her feeling for the

unfortunate of her sex that made her sensitive to the position of women generally and anxious that their interests should be guarded by law; she felt very keenly about the inequalities that then existed, and she was a supporter of granting the suffrage to women very much for this reason.

My mother hardly ever made incursions into public print, but she was on one occasion so annoyed by what she considered the unjust way in which the question was being dealt with by men who ought to have known better that she was constrained to write as follows:

" *To the Editor of ' The Times '*

"*February 16th,* 1909.

" SIR,

"Will you permit a constant reader of *The Times* to add a few lines to what has recently appeared in your columns on the question of Woman Suffrage?

" I am now in my 84th year, and have paid rates and taxes since my widowhood for upwards of 30 years.

" During that period I have had, roughly speaking, 40 men in my service, all of whom have had the opportunity of exercising their influence on the government of our country. I have three sons, all of whom have not only served their country with success and distinction, but have also attained to positions of pre-eminence in their different professions.

" Until they reached manhood and were able to exercise their right of voting, I had no direct or indirect means of expressing myself as a citizen of the Empire which I was training my sons to serve. Although I have exercised my right of voting for school board and county council, I have never had an opportunity of expressing my views on the laws these bodies are appointed to administer.

" Though I am aware that there are foolish

women as well as foolish men, such as the women Sir Edward Clarke described, I have not during my long life come in close contact with either.

"On the other hand, I have had a very extensive acquaintance with women of all classes who have served their day and generation nobly, and whose inclusion on the roll of voters would have been not only an honour but a strength to their country.

"I am, Sir, your obedient servant,
             "OCTOGENARIAN."

My father had purchased a small property in Perthshire near Gleneagles, the original home of his ancestors, and though the permanent residence had to be in Edinburgh (Charlotte Square) owing to his business as a Writer to the Signet, my mother persuaded him to add to the farmhouse and make another home there. The house was added to from time to time as occasion

required. Several months of the year were
always spent at Cloan ; and some time after
our father's death it was made our only
residence. It was a great interest to our
parents to plant, drain, and improve the
place and make paths through the woods.
The extensive view of the Grampians—for
the house faces north-west—is one of which
our mother never tired, and she always
loved to look at the sunsets. In the later
days her bed had often to be moved from
the south window to the west, in order to
see them better. The little town near
(Auchterarder) was of constant interest to
her, and for all the inhabitants whom during
seventy years' residence she came to know
through their forbears as well as themselves, she had the deepest concern. The
annual gatherings of the children of the
place, which continued until the Great War
made such parties impossible, gave both to
her and to our father while he lived the
greatest pleasure. And our father, when

MY MOTHER IN MIDDLE LIFE.

able, used in summer to hold services on Sunday evenings in a barn converted into a hall.[1]   Our mother had at one time a Sunday school for the children in the cottages around, and later on gatherings for members of the Scotch Girls' Friendly Society, of which she was President ; and when unable to meet the members in person she wrote each year a letter to greet them, which was always highly valued.   Every effort for the good of the place had her sympathy and help, so far as she could give it, and it may truly be said that she was looked on as a mother to the people.   And as very many of the people of the district have emigrated and made their homes elsewhere, there were constant communications with Canada, Australia, and other over-seas dominions.

It is difficult to say much of my mother's later life—the events are many of them too recent.   Her life in the earlier days in Edin-

---

[1] The hall was rebuilt and used for many different sorts of gatherings.   During the War it was a hospital.

burgh was a busy one. The children by
adoption grew up, married, or scattered,
but she had six of her own—five sons and
a daughter. The first boy died in infancy
—and this was a great trial. The third, an
extraordinarily clever and interesting boy
with a passion for music, died of diphtheria
at the age of sixteen, two years before his
father. This almost overwhelmed her, for
she was bound up in him and he in her.
She and the beloved Perthshire nurse,
Betsey Ferguson, better known as " Baba,"
who spent most of her life with us, nursed the
boy in days when trained nurses were hard
to find. My mother herself took diphtheria,
and for a time suffered from diphtheritic
paralysis while we were living in the lake
country, where we went for change of air.
Next year she lost her eldest brother and his
two daughters through a railway accident.
Then came our father's death when her
youngest son was twelve and the eldest
surviving son twenty. And after that there

were forty-eight years of widowhood till she reached her hundred and first year.

My father was not literary or political, being interested mainly in religious matters outside his own work as a lawyer. But that work, which meant managing a number of estates, most of them owned by family connexions of his own, brought our mother into touch with a good deal of country life, and they often paid visits together. He and she rode about at Cloan while he was able, and she enjoyed this immensely. She also went with her husband to remote hamlets, where in some little schoolroom or church he would speak to the people on Sunday evenings. She was entirely in sympathy with him in the religious work, and it was a pleasure to ride or drive to these places, where both were always welcomed. Then both were great walkers, and the children were brought up to be the same, so that expeditions to the tops of hills and over moors were frequent. Town life never appealed to our mother. Edinburgh she never cared for; the society seemed to her stiff and cold, and she found her greatest pleasure in getting to the country and being with her children.

After 1877, when our father died, it was possible to live more entirely in the country, though there were frequent visits to London, where she often took a house for the winter or spring. Also one winter was passed in Paris, and another in Rome, and during both visits my mother carried on the painting she loved so well. During her husband's life journeys had been made abroad, but they were necessarily of short duration owing to his work.

As to her later life, there was a long time—about twenty years—of ill-health. She had had an unwonted number of accidents, a bad fall from a horse in her early married life, and two serious carriage accidents later. Whether these affected her or not, she suffered extremely from neuritis following an attack of rheumatic fever in 1893. Visits to Bath were beneficial, but the enemy could not be conquered. The acute pain indeed vanished, but the lower limbs were rendered incapable of performing their function, and the last twelve years or so were passed in her room or bed. This would have been trying to most people, and it was to her, for she loved her garden and fresh air and beautiful scenery, and she longed to be out. But with infinite courage she faced the situation, read, wrote, and received visitors and kept herself in touch —and more than in touch—with the great world.

Of course the work of her children was what was most in her mind, and as that followed very varying directions it opened large fields of interest to her. She was a wonderful correspondent, and with her eldest son she kept up a daily correspondence for fifty years. Her beautifully written letters were a source of great gratification to her correspondents, and are carefully preserved by many of them. They went to relatives and friends abroad as well as at home, and hence she became a centre for all of them— a link which united those who had made their homes elsewhere with the rest of the family. The letters will not reproduce well in print, being as they are full of the personal element that made them so precious to the recipients.

Her eldest son had chosen the law as his profession, to her great pleasure, as her connexions were largely legal, and it was a special delight to her that he twice occupied the position of Lord Chancellor. It was the position her grand-uncle had held for twenty-five years, and her brother had married the sister of another Lord Chancellor (Lord Herschell), so that she felt it was a sort of family possession. So much so that, as she used laughingly to say, the nurse spoken of before, who was a second mother to all her children, set her charge on the

Always journaing affec^{tt} Mother
Mary ♁Haldane

MY MOTHER IN HER EIGHTY-FIRST YEAR.

From a picture by Thomas Graham, R.S.A.

Portrait by Henry Dixon & Son, London.

woolsack, and told him that "if he was a good laddie and learned his lessons he would one day be there by right!" Before he held that office he had been for six and a half years Secretary of State for War, and my mother seemed to be as much at home amongst the generals as the civilians, and was in her element when manœuvres were carried on round Cloan and many distinguished soldiers were present.

Then came the War with all its attendant sufferings, and the loss to her of three beloved grandsons. But sorrowing as she was, her courage never failed, and she was certain that things would work out for good. To one, high in Government service, but getting on in years, who said that he would not live to the end and that the end was uncertain, she exclaimed that she had every hope of seeing a glorious conclusion to the struggle, and victory crowning our efforts, even though she was more than twenty years his senior. She used to tell us that her father's words to her on her marriage day had been fulfilled: "Thou shalt see thy children's children, and peace upon Israel."

There was, indeed, a time of trial in attacks made on one of her family who was placed in a position in which he could not for the time reply to them. But though she deeply felt the injustice of these attacks, she was certain that this country would soon realize their injustice, and this it did in no uncertain way long before her death.

In regard to another son whose interests were scientific, she was equally eager to hear about his work as well as of that of his son, her grandson, especially as the work of both was on lines similar to that of her brother who died at Oxford in 1905. She was above all concerned with my brother's work regarding the safety of miners and divers, and rejoiced that his science had such practical application to the lives of men.

Her youngest son, who carried on his father's business in Edinburgh, made his country home on the neighbouring property of Foswell across the glen from Cloan, and the presence of the family there added greatly to the interest and joy of her life.

The grandchildren, when they returned from school or college, or from their country's service by sea or land, always made their way first to the much-loved grandmother's room—the " Chamber of Peace " to so many. She was almost as much to them as she was to her own children, and they all adored her.

My mother often said she was blessed beyond others in her perfect happiness in regard to her family—children, grandchildren, and great-grandchildren. There was never a rift between them, and those who were joined to it by marriage were as beloved and as devoted as the others. It seemed to us that we had an ideal family

15

life, and that she was its mainspring. Every
Christmas there was, as far as possible,
a family gathering, and in Scottish fashion
we " saw in " the New Year together as
a family—she praying for a blessing upon
it and us.

For those who served her she had true
affection, and she kept in touch with those
who left her service for marriage or otherwise. She constantly spoke of how much
she owed to those, her real friends, and it
was a trial to both when they had to part.
She loved to see their dresses when a party
was in prospect. Indeed, she enjoyed seeing
nice clothes always, and used to say, " Never
visit an invalid in your old things ; it cheers
them to see something bright." When going
about she always wore the best materials
and real lace or embroidery for caps or
underclothing. Her pink quilt, ribbons, and
the jackets knitted by a constant and
loved friend are present to the memory of
all her visitors when she was confined to

bed, as is the lace head-dress that became her so well and draped the beautiful white hair in its long plaits.

My mother's sense of humour was keen, and it often saved the situation in time of tension. A lady in the district tells how they had one evening been walking home from a Girls' FriendlySociety meeting, when, by some mistake, the carriage had not met her. It was Hallowe'en night, then observed in rather tempestuous fashion; they met many "Guisers" with blackened faces and strange attire, and my mother bowed and smiled to all and enjoyed it so much.

In later years her devoted sick nurse, Miss Elsie Minty, endeavoured to preserve her patient from visitors who overstayed the prescribed time of their visits, and in this she had a hard task, for even the "Dragon" (as my mother used to call her) was often nonplussed by her when in the midst of a interesting and engrossing conversation. She had amusing names for

the things around her, and all of her gifts,
whether shawls, cushions, or coverlets, were
called by the names of their donors, so that
she never forgot who had given her any
particular thing.

My mother was fond of music and loved
the sonatas of Beethoven and Mozart, and
a little piano in her bedroom was a great
source of pleasure. She drew as long as she
possibly could, even in bed, and she liked
to read books on art such as Winckelmann's.
She was an admirable reader aloud, just as
had been her father, and in former days she
read in the winter evenings nearly all the
classical novels—some of them more than
once. Among her favourites were Scott,
Jane Austen, the Brontës, Dumas, George
Eliot, Hawthorne, Thackeray, and, above
all, Dickens. I think the enjoyment of
these books was enhanced by the fact that
they were kept from her in youth. She
used to tell how when *Pickwick* first
appeared the characters were so popular

that they were represented in sugar, and that on one occasion, to the children's delight, a Twelfth Cake arrived adorned with images of Mr. Pickwick and his friends. The delight was short-lived, for, owing to its decoration, the cake was confiscated.

Her knowledge of the Scriptures was wonderful, and her reading of the Bible, in deep sonorous tones, can never be forgotten by those who heard it. I don't think I ever heard anyone read the great chapters of the Prophets more beautifully. And the reason of this was that, just as in prayer—always extempore—she forgot herself entirely and thought only of the greatness of her theme and the God she was addressing.

She never dreaded old age. " I can't feel old," she so often in later years said, " it has been the happiest part of my life. As we near the horizon our vision alters and the work given us to do is different from that of earlier years; therefore, there is

nothing to fear." Nor did she dread death.
" It is but a casting off of the old garments
to enter on a higher life." " It is all peace;
I am quite content, it is just a falling
asleep." On the other hand, she was just as
conscious of the value of life. " Life is so
full of interest," as she constantly exclaimed.

The 100th birthday seemed to the outside world to be a culminating point in
her long life. It was certainly a wonderful
occasion. The people of the town made
a presentation, which was brought to her
bedside by the Provost and Town Clerk;
the representatives of the Girls' Friendly
Society brought their address and other
presents, and she was surrounded by flowers
and all sorts of gifts, besides having many
hundred telegrams and letters coming from
the King and Queen down to the humblest
of their subjects. It was good that she
could enjoy this and the family gathering
and hear about the opening of an Institute
for young men and women whose welfare

concerned her much, and of her birthday
cake with its one hundred candles at the
neighbouring poorhouse.

But from this time on weakness grew
upon her, and it became evident to us all
that the end was approaching. Six weeks
later—on May 20th, 1925—she passed peacefully away. She had made all arrangements
for the simple service conducted by the
Rev. Mr. Todd and the ministers of the town,
and for the singing of her favourite hymn,

> "Oh Love that will not let me go,
> I rest my weary soul on Thee,"

composed by an old acquaintance, the blind
Dr. Matheson. Then her own people laid
her image on the lorry that was to take her to
Gleneagles Station, the wreaths following on
another lorry, and the long line of mourners
followed that, children, grandchildren, and
friends. We passed through the darkened
town with its flag half-mast and its sorrowing
people—for all truly sorrowed for one many
of the younger of them barely knew in

person, but all loved. The railway servants asked to be allowed to help in carrying her to her last resting-place through the police-lined road to the old West Kirkyard in Edinburgh where her husband and boys were laid. The Moderator of the Church of Scotland, then in Assembly, met the procession; the Rev. Dr. Duncan and the Rev. Dr. Ross, friends of long standing, conducted the short services at the grave and in the beautiful little Memorial Chapel close by.

NOTE BY HER ELDEST SON

III

NOTE BY HER ELDEST SON

I WISH to try to set down my impressions of my mother in the last years of her life, the years in which she was physically too much of an invalid to leave her room, but was mentally at what seemed to me her highest. Apart from her inability to move about, partial deafness was her only hindrance in the freest communication with her children.

To me the striking feature through the dozen years of which I write was my mother's steady growth in mental stature. This seemed to increase in every year. She was not what would be popularly called a learned or very clever woman. But her outlook and mental grasp were widening to the end steadily. She read extensively, in various languages, and her reading included difficult

philosophical books, as well as memoirs
and histories. Whether she took in all of
the details in these books, sometimes intri-
cate, it was not easy to tell. But it was
clear that she had grasped the substance
not only of what she read, but of the things
that had been said to her by remarkable
visitors to Cloan with whom she delighted
to hold conversations. She conveyed the
sense that she was genuinely looking at
things from a high point of view, which
reached not only to the things set down but
over them. Her mental activity was great
and its range was wide.

Deeply religious, she was yet never
narrow. The old doctrines with which she
was familiar were for her the symbols in
which she approached what she grasped
as being higher than what the symbols could
express. She was not troubled by speculative
doubts. Above these she seemed to have
risen to a standpoint from which the substance of things unseen appeared to introduce

itself unhindered by difficulties. Death had
no terrors for her. It was but an event
essential to the completion of life. She did
not dwell on pictorial imaginings of another
life. What she sought for was rather to
hold fast to the highest quality in this one,
where the human and the divine were never
for her shut off from each other. The
presence of God was foundational. But her
faith in Him was a living faith. Hers was
no abstract mind. In the person of Christ
she had always an intense sense of God
and Man as one. This was constantly
before her, and no doctrine was of value if
it did not express this, which was a supreme
fact of her experience.

Thus she was intensely religious, with
expressions for her religion that were
characteristic of her mind. Of what these expressions meant the children were keenly
conscious. But her views were never thrust
on them. She claimed liberty of thought,
and she accorded it equally freely. No

apparent aberrations in her children from
tradition surprised or distressed her.   For
from the widest point of view she saw the
truth present notwithstanding the form of
its expression.

All sorts of people used to come to the
house, and she was always anxious to see
them.   They used to leave her room impressed by her grasp of realities.   In return
she estimated them by their possession of
this kind of grasp.   She never judged
harshly.   In the learned and in the humble
she looked for the same sort of quality.
She was a fine judge of whether it was
present.   She liked to see much of her
children at her bedside, and to know all
they were trying to do, great or small.
Their pursuits were varied, but into these
various pursuits she loved to enter.   She
was a perfect mother;   our only anxiety
was to appear before her as worthy of her
great love for us. Whether we were engaged
in country life, or in household matters, or

in public work, or in philosophy, or in
science, she always seemed equally intereſted
in our efforts. She did not fail to discrimi-
nate between our visitors, but she was never
contemptuous in her criticisms. But I used
to feel that for some of them she was a
formidable person to encounter, whether
they fully realized it or not.

In the people round about, in Auchterarder, for inſtance, she maintained an intereſt
which had been keen when she could go
about, and which never flagged after she
ceased to be able to move. She delighted
in summoning them to consultations. Her
day was rarely unbroken by interviews.
These did not seem to tire her. She found
in those who came what she wanted, and if
they asked her for counsel or help it was
freely given. Her old servants she watched
over affectionately and kept up her close
friendship with them.

In her attire, whether there were visitors
or not, she was neat and exact. She had

always cared for beauty, and she liked her
clothes to look well, even when she could
only sit up in bed. Even with her children
themselves she never liked to be found
untidy. She wrote, as well as received, a
great many letters. Over the composition
of what she wrote, and her own handwriting,
she took much pains. Everything in her
life was ordered. Even the arrangements
for her own simple funeral she herself had
made, and she had insisted in discussing
them with us, long before the end came.
No one treated more thoroughly death as a
natural and necessary part of life, to be
prepared for like every other event. When
it came to her it came as a profound sorrow
for her children. For them much of the
basis of life was swept away. But the
sorrow was lightened by the preparation
of their minds for it through the years
before it descended. She wished this to be
so, and, if there was no trace of anything
morbid in her language about it, she had

succeeded in making her passing one to be looked for as the completion of her life. " I rest in God " were her favourite words. They were the words uttered by her mother when she was dying, sixty years before our mother herself died.

For me to talk with my mother was not always a simple thing. For she liked to direct the conversation to the past, rather than keep to the present, and to bring back pictures which might not easily fit into the period in which we lived. But the difficulty of appreciating this desire on her part quickly diminished as she brought out the identity of the best ideas of these early days with the substance of those of to-day. For her father, who was a profoundly religious man, she had a great reverence, and she used to speculate on what turn his mind would have taken had he been born just a few years later and remained under the influence of his contemporary at Oriel, Keble. The story of the Oxford Movement

17

was always deeply interesting to her, and she read and re-read Dean Church's book on it. She had no narrowness. The Church of England, the Presbyterian Church, the Baptists, and Plymouth Brethren, among whom she had been brought up, all appealed to her in different ways. They were the aspects which a general spiritual organization presented to her.

Thus she grew to have many friends, and very real and attached friends. With many of these she corresponded regularly to the end of her life. They felt in their different ways that whether she agreed with them or not she understood them.

But it was not only on the religious side that she attracted people. There came to Cloan and talked with her a variety of those who held foremost places in literature and in public life. Meredith, Barrie, Gosse, Whitehead, Hume Brown, Pringle Pattison in literature, and Lord Roberts, Sir Ian Hamilton, Lord Ypres, and many other soldiers, knew her well. Among public men Asquith, Edward Grey, John Dillon, Morley, Ramsay MacDonald, and a variety of those occupying high places used to visit her. Of the archbishops, bishops, and eminent divines of the other churches the list was long. I think that each felt that she had as much that was real to say to him as he had to say to her.

She was accessible, too, to all the neighbours, and they liked to talk with her over local affairs. Of these she had a wide knowledge, which she was keen to keep up-to-date. Her sense of humour in her intercourse with them and with her children was strong. She said good things when we were least looking for them, and she looked out for comedy more than for tragedy. Everything came to light with the background of her own character to make it stand out. That character did not change, and it always appeared. It showed itself in a clear view of every situation and in a strong will. A decision once come to was not easily shaken. Her mind was never doubtful even about where the things in the house were. She had a marvellous memory for where they could be found—books, articles of furniture, clothes—she remembered when she had last been able to move about and look at them, and she seemed in her old age to visualize what she had known of her possessions.

Of character she was an acute yet not unkindly judge—both in women and in men. She had a strong sense of what a " lady " ought to be like, and she recognized the natural-born lady as readily among the humble as among the great. As to men, she had an instinctive sense of whether their knowledge was real or superficial. I rarely knew her to be deceived in an estimate. To talk with and to understand those of foreign nationality was congenial to her. Of insularity she had not a trace.

A long experience of daily and sustained

personal intercourse has now come to an end for her children. The break is great, but it is not to be wondered at if a tradition has entered so deeply into their lives that it does not seem as though time could weaken it.

LETTERS AND IMPRESSIONS

IV

LETTERS AND IMPRESSIONS

In looking over my mother's correspondence
there are, outside the many bundles of
family letters, full of love and devotion, a
large number which are of interest—letters
from men of affairs as well as from those
whose lives may have been equally valuable
in their private spheres. One knows that
in themselves tributes to the memory of any
individual are apt to be unsatisfactory to
the general reader, but it may be admissible
to quote from some of these, and especially
from letters (including a few of her own)
in so far as they have bearing on her own
character and qualities.

There is a touch of the humour, so constantly found in her talk, in this note to
the late Dr. Alexander Whyte, with whom

there was a long-standing joke regarding
his and his wife's custom of talking of her
as " the Eagle " :

"CLOAN, AUCHTERARDER.
October 31st, 1910.

" The Old Eagle returns her best thanks
with her kindest regards to the very
Reverend Principal, who has been so good
as to send her the Programme of his Classes
for the Winter.   The subjects are of great
interest to her.

" The Ancient Bird is glad to inform the
Principal that her wings have been strengthened by his visit, and that of his beloved
wife, and her heart cheered by the good
words he dropped at Cloan.   She hopes
ere long to recover sufficient energy to do
what work may lie in her path for her Lord
and Master.   Her prayers will unite with
many others for a great blessing to follow
the classes of 1910–1911."

Many of the letters date from war time,

and there are a number from Lord Ypres
(then Sir John French), of which this is an
example written in a time of great anxiety
and stress :

"HEADQUARTERS, BRITISH ARMY.
August 16*th,* 1915.

"DEAR MRS. HALDANE,

"We had a delightful visit from
Lord Haldane a week or two ago, and
it gave me keen pleasure to hear from
him that you were well and that you
were sometimes kind enough to speak
of me.

"I want to send a short line to thank
you for those kind thoughts. I shall never
forget the happy hours I have spent at
Cloan or the many interesting talks we
have had there together. Do you remember
our conversation about *Northumberland*—a
county in which we are both interested ?
It makes me feel a little sad to contrast
those quiet happy peaceful days with the

truly terrific experiences of this past twelve
months.

" When I have occasion to address bodies
of men out here—which I do as often as
circumstances permit—I always tell them
I was never so proud of belonging to the
British Empire as I am now. If any war
in the world can ever have been called a
' Soldiers ' War it is this. The Empire has
been in danger and has been saved—not by
Strategists, Tacticians, and Generals—but
by the glorious gallantry, devotion, and
self-sacrifice of the British soldier in the
ranks.

" Personally I feel we have still a terribly
arduous task in front of us which will
take many more months to complete, but I
am absolutely confident as to the final and
ultimate success which we shall attain.
More than once in the last twelve months I
have been in terrible doubt of this, but
that has passed.

" Now again thanking you, dear Mrs.

Haldane, for your kind thought of me, and
with best wishes and remembrances,
    " Believe me,
        Yours very sincerely,
           J. D. P. FRENCH."

My mother herself in the same year
speaks of the War in her annual letter to the
company of young women over which she
presided for so long.

" Another year of pressing care and
anxiety has opened upon us, and we 'are
having more and more to leave all things
to the guidance of our Father in Heaven
and to His wisdom alone.   When His time
comes to give us rest and peace, nothing can
withstand His purpose or power. ' He
speaks and it is done,' and He brings to
pass wonderful things in His own way and
time. . . . In the midst of this great sorrow
light has shone—the light of the knowledge
of the glory óf God in the face of Jesus
Christ.   This is, after all, the best blessing

we can have. . . . Never in my long life
have I heard the Voice and seen His finger so
plainly as at present, in bringing near to us all
the immensity of His love and the essential
importance of recognizing that Voice and
His almighty power."   And in another letter
written after the Peace, she points out that
there is another warfare to be faced, and that
we have to try to bring about peace between
man and man and do our utmost to bring the
whole world into unison once more.   "Love
is of God, and hatred must be put far from
us, hard as the saying is."

This is a later letter, which I am allowed
to quote, from Sir James Barrie, written
after paying my mother a visit and expressing
the feelings which he had for her:

"ADELPHI TERRACE HOUSE,
STRAND, W.C.2.
September 15th, 1924.

" DEAR MRS. HALDANE,

"You have a 'personality' if ever
anyone had.   I never thought to see the

day when I could be in a house with
the Lord Chancellor without thinking him
the dominant figure (and Miss Haldane
is pretty good at personality also), but
I tell you plain you bowl them over.
I believe I went a drive with her and
a walk with him, but you swallowed
them up (Aaron's rod); and in my memory
Cloan consists of you. I see you vividly
knitting that shawl (to which my com-
pliments) and looking the dearest person
I have seen for years and years. You
really do make the intruder into that
serene room feel more hopeful about the
world. Some of the loveliest lines in
English poetry are very like you. It
would not be bad to call you an ode
to immortality. Of course I am using
strong language, but this is frankly a
love letter. I know a great deal more
about your son now. I know, for in-
stance, who is his ' spiritual home.' My
love to all at Cloan, and ' graters,' as the

schoolboys say, to myself for having been there.

"Yours affectionately,
J. M. BARRIE."

And on the occasion of her hundredth birthday there are so many. This is from the Archbishop of Canterbury, an old and deeply valued friend :

"LAMBETH PALACE, S.E.
April 7th, 1925.

"MY DEAR MRS. HALDANE,

"I am painfully conscious of wrong-doing in adding this rivulet to the flood which will pour in upon Cloan this week. And to sin with one's eyes open is grave indeed. But selfishly I cannot refrain.

"This is *my* birthday. I am 77, and when I saw the light in 1848 [in a week of Continental hurly-burly and of Chartist disorder at home] you were already a well-grown-up lady four years past her 'teens.

MY MOTHER IN HER HUNDREDTH YEAR.

Portrait by Olive Edis, F.R.P.S.

Yet somehow I never can get myself to
regard *you* as being nearly so old as *I feel*.
Whenever I talk to you I find a well-spring
of buoyant thought and an easy readiness
in handling the memories of the past which
I admire but cannot rival. And will you
let me say to you that your quiet gift of
sure touch upon the deepest things has been
to me, many a time, a spur and an inspira-
tion. I like to thank you for it now.
Sometimes when I find myself plunged
perforce in the 'strife of tongues,' and
perhaps rather frightened and depressed by
the sense of inability to guide things as one
would, I have recalled simple words of
yours about the Guide and Keeper of our
souls and have gratefully reminded myself
of your assurance that you do not forget us
in your prayers.

"' What a many ' people in difficult places,
or with hard steering to do in rough water
. and rough weather, you must in these long
decades have been thus uplifting, though

19

they knew it not. I should like you to know that one at least of these weather-beaten folks pays to you in his own thoughts and prayers the meed of gratitude which you have earned.

"And another thing. We are in happy touch with those who, in the middle life or beyond it, are now exercising from your home or its outposts the sort of influence which *tells* in fields social or political or scientific, and who owe their power of straightness and of forcefulness in no small part to what they learned from a Mother whom we can all of us thank for what she has done and is still doing for each. In the truest sense ' Her children arise and call her blessed.'

"I trust you, my dear friend, to pardon all this, for it comes from my heart.

"I am venturing to send you a little book—the ' textbook ' of my master and prophet and friend for nearly forty years— Dr. Westcott. I think you will find in it some thought which will be after your mind.

" May our Lord Himself have you in His keeping now and always.

" I am your affectionate and grateful friend,

"RANDALL CANTUAR."

.On seeing the portrait which appeared in the newspapers at that time, another friend, Principal Sir George Adam Smith, expressed his feelings in the beautiful words to be found in Ecclesiasticus (xxvi. 17) :

As the Lamp that shineth on the Holy Candlestick
Is the beauty of the face in ripe age.

In her case that beauty became accentuated and not diminished as the years passed on.

Another said, with reference to the birth-day cake with its one hundred candles : " What a blessing came one hundred years ago with Mrs. Haldane ! It is now fifty years since I first got to know and reverence her, and in all the years that followed her friendship was one of God's best gifts to me."

One would like to quote also from the many appreciations of her character which reached us after the end, but it is difficult to select. Those from men and women who had cared for her and who are settled far away over the seas are as interesting as any.

From Canada one writes : " We will all miss her. She seemed to have had a part in all our lives in Auchterarder, and I am sure it is a sorrowing town to-night."

And, again, from " an old little girl " in the United States :

" I saw twelve years ago Lord Haldane review the cadets at West Point, New York ; but the parade was obliterated to me. I saw only rows and rows of boys and girls tripping up to Cloan, tinnies hung round our necks by tape. I remember well I refused from my mother an old piece of tape for my tin, and did not budge till she went to buy the new piece. Nor shall I ever forget Mr. Haldane standing on a chair telling us he was happy to meet us, sorry to part, but would be happy to meet again. A hundred thanks for those happy moments."

A letter from New Zealand, which reached her just before she passed away from a much-loved grandson by adoption, says :

"You don't know what a joy your letters are here in this out-of-the-world corner, not only on account of the news in them, but also because of your wise and kindly comments on public affairs and people and the example you set us all of calmness, patience, and trust in God. I suppose none of your grandchildren out here failed to be influenced by you as they came to years of discretion, and yet you were confined to your room fourteen thousand miles away ! "

Mr. Cairns, the Provost of Auchterarder, put into words the feeling of her immediate neighbours before asking the members of the Town Council to observe a brief silence The Provoſt said :

"It seems but yeſterday since we were congratulating Mrs. Haldane on attaining her hundredth birthday, and to-night we are mourning her loss—a loss which we all feel as a community, and which will find an echo throughout our whole country. Mrs. Haldane was a remarkable personality. Possessed of rare talents, she used them for the higheſt ends. *Noblesse oblige* had no idle meaning for Mrs. Haldane. All her gifts were laid upon the altar of service ; all her talents were laid out to usury. She was a great example to every rank and condition of the people. The chief features of her charaćter were sympathy and graciousness. Meeting and talking with her was an unforgettable privilege which could not be analysed or communicated, and her sympathy overflowed. The dumb creation, too, found in her a friend. In the dogs' cemetery at

Cloan, where their household pets are buried, a stone is erected, with this text from the Book of Proverbs : ' Open thy mouth for the dumb.' The text was chosen by Mrs. Haldane herself, and it was characteristic of her sympathy for all living things. And now that she has quitted the house of her earthly pilgrimage for the building not made with hands, she leaves behind her the fragrant memory of a life lived for ever in her ' Great Taskmaster's ' eye."

The following is written by a friend of the last eight years of my mother's life, Miss Violet Markham (Mrs. Carruthers), whose annual visits were the source of much pleasure :

" Mrs. Haldane was already a tradition to me before I paid my first visit to Cloan in the autumn of 1917. She was then in her ninety-third year, and had been unable for a long time past to leave her couch. Cloan, her Perthshire home, stands among wooded slopes where the low range of the Ochils rises from the valley of the Earn. From the windows of Mrs. Haldane's room on the first floor you look for miles across the broad strath with its farms and cornfields, till the view is bounded by the Grampian Hills blue and distant on the western horizon. In the foreground lies the little town of Auchterarder, bound by many happy and intimate ties with the Haldane family. Whatever the weather, that room always left upon a visitor a sense of warmth and sunshine.   It was filled, indeed, by the presence of the woman, old in years but young in spirit, who lay among her pillows. What a truly regal figure she was, this mistress of Cloan, to whose quality Time year by year seemed to bring some fresh gift and to take none away ! White hair fell softly above the noble brow and finely moulded features, while delicious vanities of lace and pink ribbons framing the face added a purely feminine touch to her appearance. She was working at a pale pink crochet shawl as I came in, but looked up with a smile of welcome which banished all shyness in the newcomer. Whatever physical limitations age might have imposed, it was clear at a glance that here was a spirit still keen and alert. Sunshine and flowers, the picture of those she loved about her, peace, tenderness, serenity, withal a very definite sense of power and authority—such was the first impression of her bedside. In years to come that impression was to widen and deepen in countless ways.

"Friends of far older standing than mine have paid tribute to her memory. But Mrs. Haldane had the true mark of greatness, inasmuch as the light within her shone from many varied facets, and different people caught the light from different sides. No written word can do justice to her personality; every sketch is necessarily incomplete. But it may be of interest to future generations of Haldanes to read the im-

20

pressions, however fugitive, of those who had been brought into personal touch with their great ancestress. The autumn pilgrimage to Cloan was a factor in many lives, and those of us who were privileged to climb the turret staircase found in that upper chamber a shrine to which we came to renew our faith and strength.

" Mrs. Haldane was unique. The charm and graciousness of her old age adorned, but did not hide, her massive intellect and personality. No woman has ever given me so great an impression of strength. One who saw her in her last sleep spoke of the majesty written on the calm face. ' She looked as though she might have ruled an Empire,' and I could well believe it. Had she been born fifty or sixty years later what mark might she not have left on the world ? But in 1825 woman was cabined, cribbed, confined. Conventionality and custom hemmed her in at every turn. To vary a remark made by Matthew Arnold, a spiritual east wind was blowing, and the women of the best intellects could not flower. Further, the Burdon-Sandersons and the Haldanes of that day, held, and held with fervour, evangelical principles in which their children were rigidly brought up. Mary Burdon-Sanderson as a girl and a young woman had to struggle against limitations almost incredible to our own rising generation. She had in her the quality which during the Middle Ages would have gone to the making of a great saint; for saints are always very practical people in the practical things of life. Like St. Catherine of Siena, I could see her dealing faithfully with Popes and Cardinals, or like St. Theresa, directing with crisp authority the multifarious affairs of a scattered order. Or, again, she might have been a Deborah—judging her people in peace, leading them to victory in war.

" But in her youth there was little escape even for a powerful and gifted intellect from the shackles of the pre-Victorian period, aggravated as they were by a rigid orthodoxy in religious matters. It was a great experience to hear her talk of those days. She told me once of all she had endured as a child from the tyranny of a governess—another product of the age now mercifully extinct—who outraged her sense of truth and justice by insisting that she must have broken *all* the Ten Commandments severally and collectively. The spirit within her as a girl was early up and doing, but even her strong wings could carry her on no adequate flight. Determined spirits by hook or by crook achieved education : the culture wrung at such cost was often of higher quality than that achieved by the modern young woman to whom every advantage of university life lies open. Mary Burdon-Sanderson must have had a remarkable gift for languages. She studied German, French, and Italian, as well as Latin and Greek, and the knowledge of them remained with her through life. But she felt deeply the humiliation and impotence of woman's position when man alone was the fount of grace and favour; and the reasons which determined her marriage to a widower with five children were characteristic of her whole attitude towards life.

" ' I had made up my mind that I should never marry,' she told me once. ' In my youth a married woman had no more position than a cat, and it was my intention to be a missionary and devote my life to the care of the heathen. But when Mr. Haldane wished to marry me I felt it was my duty to obey the nearer call and devote my life to him and his motherless children.' It was in her home and through her children that her character found its full expression; its greatness has been reflected in other lives.

" What was the secret of this greatness? Here we touch mainsprings of life and character of which it is not easy to speak—sanctities on which no clumsy hand should be laid. But so much has been said—and said rightly—of her intellectual gifts that I am moved to stress the spiritual quality which was the motive force of her being. As I see it, the secret of Mrs. Haldane's power was that her life was lived wholly and continuously in the presence of God. Few people could have been given a spiritual consciousness more real and more penetrating. The sense of the Divine Presence and the Divine Guidance filled her being. But this keen spiritual sense did not express itself in any narrow or obscurantist piety; it was as the poles apart from the sentimental religiosity which drives many critical spirits to turn with impatience from the practices and the patter of a conventional faith. In her shone that ' power of God and wisdom of God ' on which St. Paul lays stress as the hall-mark of the consecrated life. She drew on great reservoirs of spiritual strength unknown to the average religious experience, and her character, strong as it was gracious, had touched eternal values. During the thirty years of life granted to her beyond the Psalmist's span she had come to see many things *sub specie æternitatis*. In extreme old age she gave the impression of already living in a measure in the world beyond. The human affections were as strong as ever; her intellectual keenness for all which concerned politics, literature, and science remained undimmed. But she had lain for so long at the portals of the Hereafter that God's finger had touched her long ere she slept. Hence a certain seer-like quality in those last years which carried her through an experience crushing in its weight to many old people. For even the War could not quench her spirit.

To the last she was old but never aged. As President of the Auchterarder Girls' Friendly Society it was her habit to write a pastoral letter annually to the young people, to whom she was a great and honoured name. The final letter, written in her hundredth year, is instinct with calm virility and wide outlook. It bears no internal evidence of any kind of age, let alone failing powers. On the laſt occasion I saw her, in the autumn of 1924, she was reading Winckelmann in Italian when I went into her room. We have all known charming old ladies whose declining years were enveloped in a pleasant atmosphere of make-believe. But Mrs. Haldane was too great for the smalleſt element of sham to enter into her old age. Concessions to her physical weakness were inevitable, but her mind and her spirit adventured to the laſt without capitulations of any kind.

" Hence the tower of ſtrength she proved to others during the long agony of the War, despite the heavy trials which fell to her personal lot. Death did not spare her family. She saw with anguish young lives dear to her cut short in the promise of their youth. More poisonous ſtill was the campaign of calumny and abuse heaped on her son. Many women of her age would

have had no strength to react against a
wound so deep. The vile slanders of the
hour did not spare herself. 'They actually
said I was an illegitimate daughter of the
German Emperor,' she told me one day, her
voice full of indignation, and then humour
overcame indignation and we laughed
together over the grotesque tale. The
autumn of 1917, when I met her first, was
a very black moment in the war. There
were few hearts in which weariness and
despondency did not reign. The enthusiasms
of the early days had long since vanished.
Most people stumbled under a burthen not
only of sorrow but of crushing disillusion.
Yet in that dark hour her faith never
faltered. To sit by her side, to listen to her
calm and confident prophecy of coming
victory, was to recharge one's own waning
batteries. I can remember her gentle but
withal firm reproof when I had been guilty
of some despondent word about the future :
'But how can you doubt that God will

bring us safely through these trials?' And the look and the words would have shamed the most sorry laggard into fresh effort. Little wonder that in those days tired men and women came to Cloan and left with their strength renewed.

"Her relations with her children and grandchildren were without shadow. Few families have been united by bonds so close as those of the Haldanes of Cloan. The tie between a mother and a famous son has given rise to many tender and beautiful pages in history, but no page more tender and more beautiful than that tie between Lord Haldane and his mother. Here again we tread on ground too intimate for public gaze. In a daily correspondence of more than fifty years no pressure of public business or of abstract thought stood between the letter which, written nightly by the son from the heart of affairs in London, was read eagerly by the mother in the peaceful home

at Cloan.   Proud though she was of her
eldest son, her other children gave her cause
for pride no less deep.   Each has left his or
her mark on the life of our times.   In each
we see reflected some special quality of their
mother's character.

"What I think has been less recognized
is the part played by the children in the
evolution of the mother's character.   I
have spoken of the limitations which surrounded Mrs. Haldane's youth.   A rigid
Evangelical outlook joined to a powerful
character might have led to disaster in the
later relationships of life.   Between gifted
and able mothers and children no less gifted
and no less able the possibilities of conflict
are unlimited.   And it would be idle to
pretend that the Haldane family at one
moment were not called upon to make
some difficult adjustments.   The children
grew up with capacities and characters no
whit inferior to those of the mother, but
born in a later generation and different in

their intellectual outlook.   The breaking
away of children into new and uncharted
fields of speculation may prove a tragic
experience for the parent.   Was not Lord
Haldane sent to complete his university
training in Germany so as to avoid what
his parents regarded as the irreligious atmosphere of Oxford dominated by Jowett?
But here the essential greatness of Mrs.
Haldane's mind and character asserted itself.
She was big enough to break the bonds of
her early training, to see the justice of her
children's point of view, to wheel into line
with them.   And from this time onward
began a new phase of development which
went on continuously till the last day of her
life.   Instead of leading a forlorn existence
defending some untenable position behind
a sandbag on a barricade, she came into step
with her children and adventured with them
whole-heartedly in the treasure rooms of
the new knowledge and new ideas of our
time.

"No woman I have ever known was more filled with what Meredith calls 'the rapture of the forward view.' This enthusiasm for the future was, I think, the most remarkable feature in a remarkable character. The melancholy foible of middle and old age with its face turned backwards and its heart filled with lamentation for the blessings of the past never touched her spirit. Pessimists and croakers fared badly in the upper room at Cloan. Her face was set to the sunrise and to the future, and her faith in the infinite powers of perfection in human nature made her hold out both hands to the changes through which growth and development alone can come. The advent of the Labour Government left her not only unmoved but wholly sympathetic to the venture.

"I never saw her in the company of her grandchildren, but she would talk with pride of the rising generation of Haldanes in whom she lived to see the brilliant intellectual gifts of the family once more renewed. It would be unreasonable to pretend she was not sometimes a little puzzled by their outlook on life. But though this might be less intelligible to her than the work and ideas of her own sons and daughter, strong ties of affection as well as sympathy bound her to the younger generation and them to her. The lines written by Naomi Mitchison on her funeral are a tribute understanding and complete from a woman in the fullness of her youth to one who had fallen asleep in the fullness of age.

" I think a great and final effort of will sustained her failing strength over the hundredth birthday ; but her course was run, and the effort made she sank gently into the Everlasting Arms which had upheld her through life. From old and young, rich and poor, from King and peasant, came words of sorrow at the passing of so great a Mother in Israel. To many of us who heard the news it brought a sense of irrevocable loss, of something blessed which had gone for ever from our ken. . . .

"Let us think only with pride and thankfulness of the enduring possession of her memory. The light in the upper room has suffered no extinction. It shines on in the fuller presence of that undying Life in which we dare to hope all spirit and all purpose find fullness and renewal."

And from a different point of view an old and valued friend, Sir Edmund Gosse, expressed what he felt in a communication to *The Times* :

"At the time when she completed her hundredth year, more than a month ago, the appreciations of Mrs. Haldane were numerous and cordial, but from discretion they hardly touched upon her character. A long-time friend hesitates to join the chorus of praise to-day, but he dares come forward to drop a heart's ease on her coffin. Her mental and moral features in these last

years were so remarkable that one is tempted
to describe them as unprecedented; at all
events there is no record, that I know, of
the faculties and emotions being so vividly
preserved in extreme old age. Indeed, there
seemed to be a positive advance almost to
the very last, and it is hardly a paradox to
declare that the mind and soul of Mrs.
Haldane ripened to the very edge of her
century.

" Her character was firm, and doubtless
had known a touch of Puritan severity;
towards her end it steadily mellowed, but
rather from the action of reason than from
any softening of the will. She was profoundly religious, and to the end delighted
to discuss, but no longer with any harshness,
the strenuous tenets of her youth. She
became, not from indifference, but from
experience and benevolence, entirely tolerant.
She was accustomed to authority, but her
rule was mild and magnificent. Her solidity
of judgment was suitable to one who had

meditated much, and had loved much, and who in the course of a hundred years had come to place an entire confidence in her own judgment, which had not betrayed her.

" The bent of her intelligence was not, as might have been expected, towards philosophy, though she thought with exactitude. Discouraged by early training, her natural tendency was rather in an æsthetic direction. In her extreme old age, not without a certain felicity, she cultivated the fine arts, was poet, painter, even musician."

My mother was impressed by the words in the prophecy of Zechariah about the golden pipes which empty the golden oil out of themselves into the golden candle-sticks. " The oil," she wrote, " was to be running over. So it is with our prayers. Many a prayer that has issued from these golden pipes has been, as it were, pressed out of some of us. It may have been a half-whispered word, or no word at all, merely

22

the spirit moving. And thus it has entered those golden pipes and has been carried by them to the Throne of Grace and Peace that is ready to receive it." The very laſt letter she ever wrote had reference to this conception. She used to call the Archbishop of York (whose sermons she conſtantly read) her "Golden Candleſtick." She wrote on Good Friday, just after her hundredth birthday, these few lines :

"My dear Golden Candlestick,

"I am reſting peacefully, helped through a sharp attack of influenza by your message given to me : 'You cannot be lonely, He is always with you.' I have been carried through. Praying without ceasing for you and the Archbishop of Canterbury.

"Affeĉtionately yours and his,

"Mary E. Haldane."

We might conclude with part of the laſt of the many yearly letters to the members of the society (the Scotch Girls' Friendly Society) she loved so well, all written in her beautiful Italian handwriting. This one was sent a few months before her death, when in her hundredth year :

" I am very much struck when I read the history of our Divine Lord's life in the Gospels by the example He set us all. ' I have finished the work Thou gavest Me to do,' is recorded as His Divine utterance in prayer. His work was perfect, and in doing that work He carried out the duties of life in this world in conformity with the fulfilment of that Divine mission which was only complete when He uttered on the cross those glorious words, and ascended on high bearing the curse and suffering for the sins of His people.

" I do not expect to be long beside you, but I am anxious to present to you my very earnest wish and prayer that you should follow Him in spirit and in action who made Himself of no reputation in order to fulfil that work which His Father in heaven had given Him to do. We all have duties to perform. They may be small and may be difficult, but they are given us to do, and in doing those we must take possession of ourselves, and we shall assuredly receive our reward. I can only add my prayer and desire that you may have the same experience as I have had in witnessing the goodness of God in helping those who have followed the example of their Lord and Saviour.

" May we none of us forget this, but work while it is day, and, in doing the work set before us, glorify our Father which is in heaven. That He may continue to give you all His blessing, and enable you to do His work and will, is the prayer and wish of

" Your affectionate old President,

" MARY E. HALDANE."

LINES WRITTEN BY A GRAND-DAUGHTER, NAOMI MITCHISON

" O grave, where is thy victory ? "

1

How green the fields are,
How golden the broom,
How fine the lilies smelt
In that packed room !

2

You should have trumpets now,
And riders to ride,
Like the trumpets and white-robed ones
That came to Christian
On that other side.

3

In the red-wheeled lorries
Go strong brown horses,
That step their courses
And bear you along.
On the stretching roadway
Horse-hoofs and footsteps
Make a quiet song.

4

The birds sing shrill
Out of the beeches;
Grey smoke and brown smoke
And mists hang still
Over the lowlands;
And down the hill
And across the hollow
House folk and town folk
And farm folk follow.

5

In the Scottish houses the blinds are all down,
You go like a queen through the whole long town,
They have seen you and known you, in your works
      and your ways,
Their lives have shown you they have given you
      praise.
Rain on the pavement now, and rain in the sky,
But they come out bareheaded, to watch you go by.

Lightning Source UK Ltd.
Milton Keynes UK
UKHW011829210422
401865UK00001B/167